Acts and Resolutions
of the
General Council,
of the Choctaw Nation.

PASSED AT ITS

REGULAR SESSION

1904.

ACTS AND RESOLUTIONS OF THE GENERAL COUNCIL OF THE CHOCTAW NATION

Passed at its Extraordinary
and Regular Sessions, 1905

SR Scholarly Resources Inc.
1508 Pennsylvania Avenue · Wilmington, Delaware 19806

SCHOLARLY RESOURCES, INC.
Wilmington, Delaware • London

Reprint edition published in 1975

Library of Congress Catalog Card Number: 75-3693
ISBN: 0-8420-1884-0

Manufactured in the United States of America

Acts and Resolutions

of the

General Council,

of the Choctaw Nation.

PASSED AT ITS

REGULAR SESSION

1904.

Acts of the Choctaw Nation

OCTOBER SESSION,

1904

BILL NO. 1.

RESOLUTION AUTHORIZING THE CHAIRMAN OF CHIEF MESSAGE COMMITTEE TO APPOINT A CLERK.

Be it Resolved by the General Council of the Choctaw Nation in Regular Session Assembled:

SECTION 1. That the Chairman of the Committee on Chief Message shall appoint a clerk of said committee, whose duty it shall be to make and keep a full record of the said committee.

SEC. 2. Be it further resolved, That the clerk of said Chief Message Committee shall receive for his services the sum of four dollars ($4.00) per day; that the National Auditor shall issue his warrant for actual service, and the National Treasurer shall pay the same.

And this resolution shall take effect and be in force from and after its passage and approval.

Proposed by L. H. Perkins.

In affect by statue of limitation Oct. 13, 1904.

GREEN McCURTAIN,
P. C. C. N.

ATTEST:

J. W. CONSER,
Recording Secretary.

BILL NO. 2.

RESOLUTION AUTHORIZING THE CHAIRMAN OF FINANCE COMMITTEE TO APPOINT A CLERK.

Be it Resolved by the General Council of the Choctaw Nation in Regular Session Assembled:

SECTION 1. That the Chairman of the Finance Committe shall appoint a clerk for the said committee, whose duty it shall be to make and keep a full record of the work of said committee.

SEC. 2. Be it further resolved, That the Clerk of the said Finance Committee shall receive for his services five dollars ($5.00) per day.

That the National Auditor shall issue his warrant for actual services and the Treasurer shall pay the same; and this resolution shall take effect and be in force from and after its passage and approval.

Proposed by A. H. Reed.

In affect by statute of limitation this Oct. 13, 1904.

GREEN McCURTAN,

ATTEST: P. C. C. N.

J. W. CONSER,

Recording Secretary.

BILL NO. 3.

RESOLUTION AUTHORIZING THE CHAIRMAN OF THE COMMITTEE ON PETITIONS TO APPOINT A CLERK.

Be it Resolved by the General Council of the Choctaw Nation in Regular Session Assembled:

SECTION 1. That the Chairman of the Committee on Petitions shall appoint a clerk for the said committee, whose duty it shall be to make and keep a full record of the work of said committee.

SEC. 2. Be it further resolved, That the Clerk of the said Petition Committee shall receive for his services four dollars ($4.00) per day; that the National Auditor shall issue his warrant for actual services, and the Treasurer shall pay the same.

And this resolution shall take effect and be in force from and after its passage and approval.

Proposed by J. P. Thompson.

In affect by statute of limitation this Oct. 13, 1604.

GREEN McCURTAIN,

ATTEST: P. C. C. N.

J. W. CONSER,

Recording Secretary.

BILL NO. 4.

RESOLUTION ACCEPTING REPORT OF I. S. LOWERY, COLLECTOR FOR THE 1ST DISTRICT, C. N., FOR QUARTERS ENDING JUNE 30, 1904.

Your committee to whom was referred the report of I. S. Lowrey, district collector for the First District of the Choctaw Nation, have carefully examined the said reports in detail, and find that it covers the following quarters, to-wit:

Quarters ending September 30, 1903 - -	$1120 24
" " December 31, 1903 - - -	1937 28
" " March 31, 1904 - - -	1616 26
' " June 30, 1904 - - - -	932 52
Grand total - - - - - -	$5606 30
Less 10 per cent. - - - -	560 63
Due the Nation - - - - -	$5045 67

The total amount due the Nation is shown to be the sum of five thousand and forty-five dollars and sixty-seven cents ($5045.67). Receipts from the National Treasurer shows that this amount has been paid in, and your committee recommend the adoption of the following resolution:

"Be it resolved, by the General Council of the Choctaw Nation assembled, that the report of I. S. Lowery, collector for the First District of the Choctaw Nation, be, and the same is hereby accepted, as true and correct, and this resolution take effect and be in force from and after its passage and approval."

Proposed by James Bower, Chairman of Finance

Committee.

Approved this the 14th day of Oct. 1904.

GREEN McCURTAIN,

ATTEST: P. C. C. N.

J. W. CONSER,

Recording Secretary.

BILL NO 5.

A RESOLUTION TO DEFRAY THE EXPENSES OF THE COMMITTEE APPOINTED TO ATTEND THE FUNERAL OF CAPTAIN J. S. STANLEY.

Be it Resolved by the General Council of the Choctaw Nation Assembled:

SECTION 1. That an appropriation of fifty ($50) dollars, be, and the same is, hereby authorized and made, for the purpose of defraying the expenses incurred by the committee appointed to attend the funeral services of Captain J. S. Stanley; and the National Auditor be, and he is hereby empowered and directed to issue his warrant for that amount and the National Treasurer shall pay the same out of any other funds not otherwise appropriated.

SEC. 2. This resolution shall take effect and be in force from and after its passage.

Proposed by J. L. Ward.

Approved this the 25th day of Oct., 1904.

GREEN McCURTAIN,
P. C. C. N.

ATTEST:

JOE W. CONSER,
Recording Secretary.

BILL NO. 6.

WHEREAS, The sad intelligence of the death of our late comrade, co-worker and fellow citizen, Captain J. S. Stanley, has just been conveyed to us; and,

WHEREAS, While in life his energies were directed in the achievement of the best ends for the interest of his fellow citizens, and feeling deeply the loss we have sustained;

THEREFORE, Be it resolved by the General Council of the Choctaw Nation assembled:

That out of respect to the memory of our esteemed and honored friend, the Senate and House of Representatives, of the Choctaw Nation, now in general council assembled, adjourn at 5 p. m. this 20th day of October, and remain disolved until Monday, October 24th, at 9 a. m., and that the Principal Chief be directed to appoint a committee, consisting of two Senators and one Representative, to attend the funeral of Captain J. S. Stanley, and;

Be it further resolved, That the said committee, so appointed, convey to the members of Captain Stanley's family, the deep condolence of the Choctaw Council, in this the hour of their sad bereavment.

Proposed by J. L. Ward.

Approved this the 20th day of October, 1904.

GREEN McCURTAIN,

ATTEST: P. C. C. N.

J. W. CONSER,

Recording Secretary.

BILL NO. 7.

AN ACT AUTHORIZING THE PRINCIPAL CHIEF TO APPOINT A COMMISSION FOR THE ENROLLMENT OF NEW BORN CHOCTAWS, AND OTHER PURPOSES.

Whereas, By the terms of the supplementary agreement, the citizenship rolls of the Choctaw Nation were closed on September 25, 1902, and no children born of Choctaw Indian parentage thereafter could be enrolled; and

Whereas, Many Indian children have been borned since the above date and whose right to enrollment and participation in the division of tribal property entitles them to favorable consideration; and

Whereas, Certain delinquent Choctaws who have had a tribal status have failed to secure enrollment.

Be it enacted by the General Council of the Choctaw Nation assembled:

SECTION 1. The Principal Chief is hereby authorized to appoint a commission, composed of three members, for the purpose of enrolling such children of Choctaw parentage as have been born since September 25, 1902, and children that may be born up to and including March 4, 1906.

SEC. 2. Said commission shall also be authorized to enroll such delinquent Choctaws as heretofore have had a tribal status, and none other.

SEC. 3. The commission thus created shall be under the supervision of the Principal Chief, who shall have power to supervise the work of the Commission and revise the same from time to time, and in the exercise of this authority shall have power to canvass the list of names of the children and delinquent Choctaws received by the commission for enrollment.

SEC. 4. Be it further enacted that it shall be the duty of the Commission to investigate each case on its own merits, and shall take testimony only after it fully appears that the parents of such children have been duly enrolled, and as such their names appear upon the final rolls, as approved by the Honorable Secretary of the Interior.

SEC. 5. Upon the completion of the enrollment of new born children and delinquent Choctaws, as herein before provided, said rolls shall be delivered to the Principal Chief, who is hereby authorized to procure such legislation by Congress as to secure the final enrollment of the aforesaid new born children and delinquent Choctaws.

SEC. 6. The Principal Chief shall designate one member of the Commission as Chairman, who shall keep the records, books and papers in his custody, and shall furnish blank applications and such other necessary forms to applicants for enrollment as the Commission may deem necessary.

SEC. 7. Be it further enacted that each Commissioner under this act shall receive $1,800 per annum, as a salary, and the additional sum of $1,000 is hereby appropriated for the purpose of procuring such stationery, books, and defraying such other necessary incidental and contingent expenses of said Commission; and all payments shall be made quarterly upon the certificate of the Principal Chief to the Auditor, whose warrants the Treasurer shall pay out of any funds not otherwise appropriated.

SEC. 8. Be it further enacted that the contingent fund of the Principal Chief, in addition to that now provided by law, is hereby increased sufficent to carry the purpose of this act into effect, and an appropriation therefor is hereby made, and this act shall take effect and be in force from and after its passage and approval, and all acts and parts of acts in conflict herewith are hereby repealed.

Proposed by Daniel Webster, Chairman Choctaw Message Committee.

Approved this the 20th day of October, 1904.

GREEN McCURTAIN

ATTEST: P. C. C. N.

J. W. CONSER,

Recording Secretary.

AMENDMENT.

That line 3 in Section 1, be amended after the words "Choctaw parentage" by adding the words and "the Choctaw Freedman parentage."

Amendment proposed by W. A. Shoney.

BILL NO. 8.

RESOLUTION ACCEPTING THE REPORT OF HENRY L. SANGUIN, DISTRICT COLLECTOR FOR THE THIRD DISTRICT OF THE CHOCTAW NATION, CONVERING FOUR QUARTERS, BEGINNING THE 1ST DAY OF JULY, 1903, AND ENDING THE 30TH DAY OF JUNE, 1904.

Your committee to whom was referred the report of Henry L. Sanguin, District Collector for the Third District, Choctaw Nation, have carefully examined the same and find that it covers the four quarters, beginning the first day of July, 1903, and ending the 30th day of June, 1904. Our examination shows the total amount collected to be three thousand four hundred and ninety-seven dollars and thirty-four cents ($3,497.34); less 10 per cent., three hundred and forty-nine dollars and seventy-three cents ($349.73); due the Nation, three thousand one hundred and forty-seven dollars and sixty-one cents ($3,147.61). Receipts from the National Treasurer and warrants handed in to the Committee, show that this amount has been paid into the National Treasurer,

Therefore, We, your committee, recommend the adoption of the following resolution:

Be it Resolved by the General Council of the Choctaw Nation Assembled:

That the report of Henry L. Sanguin, District Collector for the Third District, be, and the same is hereby accepted, as true and correct, that this resolution shall take effect and be in force from and after its passage and approval.

Proposed by James Bower, Chairman of Finance Committee.

Approved this the 27th day of Oct. 1904.

GREEN McCURTAIN,
P. C. C. N.

ATTEST:

J. W. CONSER,
Recording Secretary.

BILL NO 9.

A RESOLUTION OF ADJOURNMENT.

Be it Resolved by the General Council of the Choctaw Nation Assembled:

That the present regular session of Council do adjourn Thursday, Nov. 3, 1904, at 10 o'clock a. m., and this resolution shall take effect and be in force from and after its passage and approval.

Proposed by Ed McDaniel.

Approved this, the 27th day of October, 1904.

GREEN McCURTAIN,
P. C. C. N.

ATTEST:

J. W. CONSER,
Recording Secretary.

BILL NO. 10.

A RESOLUTION ENDORSING THE ADMINISTRATION OF HON. GEORGE K. PRITCHARD, AS UNITED STATES MARSHAL FOR THE CENTRAL DISTRICT, INDIAN TERRITORY.

Whereas, The Indian, though slow of speech, is not

lacking in appreciation, and

Whereas, Honorable George K. Pritchard, the United States Marshal for the Central District, Indian Territory, has won the admiration and respect of the Choctaw people generally, through his vigorous enforcement of the law, without fear or favor; and

Whereas, The presentation of this view is so refreshing to the public generally, and the Indian in particular, that it needs to be chronicled.

Be it therefore resolved, by the General Council of the Choctaw Nation assembled:

That the thanks of this body be extended to Honorable George K. Pritchard, United States Marshal, for his uniform enforcement of the law and his manifest determination to apply but one standard to those who violate its precepts.

Be it further resolved, That a copy of this resolution be forwarded to Honorable George K. Pritchard as an evidence of the appreciation of his service by the Choctaw people.

Be it further resolved That this resolution take effect and be in force from and after its passage and approval.

Proposed by James Bower.

Approved this the 27th day of October, 1904.

GREEN McCURTAIN,

ATTEST: P. C. C. N.

J. W. CONSER,

Recording Secretary.

BILL NO. 11.

AN ACT TO RATIFY AND CONFIRM THE EMPLOYMENT OF MESSRS. M'CURTAN AND HILL, AS COUNSEL, IN GUARDIANSHIP AND ADMINISTRATION, BY THE PRINCIPAL CHIEF, AND PROVIDE COMPENSATION.

Whereas, By the following provisions of the act of Congress, approved April 28, 1904, the Arkansas guardianship and administration law was extended and put in force in the Indian Territory:

"All the laws of Arkansas, heretofore put in force in Indian Territory, are hereby continued and extended in their operation so as to embrace all persons and estates in said Territory, whether Indian, Freedman, or otherwise, and full and complete jurisdiction is hereby conferred on the District Courts in said Territory in the settlement of all estates of decedents, the guardianship of minors and incompetents, whether Indians, Freedman, or otherwise"; and

Whereas, Our people are unaccustomed to the procedure in Federal Courts, and many of them are without the means necessary to protect their interests before said tribunals and

Whereas, Unscrupulous parties, known as grafters, are taking advantage of the unfortunate condition of our people to defraud them of their property, and sometimes of the landed interests itself, under guise of guardianship or administration, procured by misrepresentation; now therefore,

Be it enacted by the General Council of the Choctaw Nation assembled:

SECTION 1. That the action of the Principal Chief

in employing Messrs. McCurtain and Hill, attorneys in Choctaw guardianship and administration in the United States Courts be, and the same is hereby ratified and confirmed.

SEC. 2. That for the services performed and to be performed by the attorneys employed in guardianship and administration, said attorneys shall receive as compensation the sum of fifteen thousand ($15,000) dollars; provided that said services shall continue to the end of the triabal government, namely: March 4, 1906, without additional compensation.

SEC. 3. That in addition to the compensation herein provided, the sum of five thousand ($5,000) dollars, per annum, or so much thereof as may be necessary, shall be allowed to said attorneys as expenses in the prosecution of guardianship and administration cases in their charge.

SEC. 4. That said attorneys are hereby required and directed to make a full and complete report to the next Council of the service rendered and the expenses incurred in each and every case where they are attorneys of record, or in which they enter an appearance in behalf of the Indian parties in interest.

SEC. 5. That a sum sufficient to carry into effect the provisions of this act are hereby set aside and made available as additional contingent fund of the Principal Chief; that for the compensation and expenses herein provided, the National Auditor shall issue his warrant quarterly, upon the certificate of the Principal Chief, and the National Treasurer shall pay the same.

SEC. 6. That this act shall take effect and be in force from and after its passage and approval.

Proposed by James Bower, Chairman of Finance Committee.

Approved this the 27th day of Oct., 1904.

GREEN McCURTAIN,
P. C. C. N.

ATTEST:

JOE W. CONSER,
Recording Secretary.

BILL NO. 12.

AN ACT VALIDATING CERTAIN NATIONAL WARRANTS.

Whereas, It developes upon the examination of the National Auditor's report for the fiscal year 1904, that said Auditor did issue national warrants to the amount of two hundred and eighty ($280) dollars upon certificates ordered by the various county clerks in the Choctaw Nation, for the expense of holding an election December 19, 1903; and,

Whereas, The National Treasurer paid said warrants upon the theory that they were regular and authorized by law; and,

Whereas, It may develop that there are a few certificates issued under similar circumstances and ought to be likewise paid.

Be it therefore enacted, by the General Council of the Choctaw Nation assembled:

SECTION 1. That said warrants, and those hereafter issued upon certificates above mentioned be, and the same are hereby declared valid; that the National Auditor is hereby authorized to issue his warrants upon presentation of the said certificates and the National Treasurer shall pay the same, out of any money not otherwise appropriated.

Proposed by James Bower, Chairman of Finance Committee.

Approved this the 27th day of October, 1904.

GREEN McCURTAIN,
P. C. C. N.

ATTEST:

J. W. CONSER,
Recording Secretary.

AMENDMENT TO SECTION 1.

Insert on the last line after the word "appropriated": "And that this act take effect and be in force from and after its passage and approval."

BILL NO. 13.

AN ACT PROVIDING FOR THE APPOINTMENT OF A COMMISSION TO NEGOTIATE WITH THE CHICKASAWS, OR THEIR REPRESENTATIVES, A SETTLEMENT OF ALL EXISTING DIFFERENCES BETWEEN THE CHOCTAWS AND CHICKASAWS, AND AN ADJUSTMENT OF ALL OTHER MATTERS OF JOINT INTEREST BETWEEN THE TRIBES.

Be it Enacted by the General Council of the Choctaw Nation Assembled:

SECTION 1. That the Principal Chief be, and he is

hereby authorized, to appoint a commission composed of three persons, of which he shall be a member and act as chairman, for the purpose of affecting a settlement upon the part of the Choctaw Nation of all existing matters between the Choctaw and Chickasaw Nations, and for the adjustment of all matters of joint interest between said tribes.

SEC. 2. That said Committee shall, upon its appointment, or as soon thereafter as is practicable, proceed to the consideration of the matters and things by this act committed to its charge, that a record of the final action, conclusions and recommendations of the joint commission shall be made and by this commission reported to the Principal Chief for transmission to the Council at its next succeeding session, either regular or extraordinary, for the Council's ratification or rejection, as to it may seem best for the interest of the Choctaw people.

SEC. 3. That the compensation for said commissioners shall be five ($5.00) dollars per day when actually engaged in the service herein provided for, and three ($3.00) dollars per day in lieu of subsistences, including transportation and other necessary and incidental expenses.

SEC. 4. That the sum of five hundred ($500) dollars, or so much thereof as may be necessary, shall be made available, and upon certificate of the Principal Chief the National Auditor shall issue his warrant and the National Treasurer shall pay the same. That the contingent fund of the Principal Chief is hereby sufficiently increased to carry into effect the provisions of this act; and this act shall take effect from and after its passage and approval.

Proposed by Daniel Webster, Chairman on Chief Message Committee.

Approved this the 27th day of October, 1904.

GREEN McCURTAIN
P. C. C. N.

ATTEST:

J. W. CONSER,
Recording Secretary.

BILL NO. 14.

MEMORIAL REQUESTING CONTINUANCE OF PRESENT CHOCTAW TOWNSITE COMMISSION UNTIL ITS WORK IS COMPLETED:

Whereas, The Choctaw Townsite Commission has received notice through the Honorable J. George Wright, U. S. Indian Inspector for the Indian Territory, that owing to lack of funds said Commission would be dissolved on or about November 1st, 1904, and;

Whereas, The work of the Commission is far from completion, and a suspension or discontinuance of the Commission at this time, would irreparably injure the interests of the Choctaw and Chickasaw Nations,

Be it Resolved by the General Council of the Choctaw Nation in Regular Session Assembled:

That it is the sense of the Choctaw people that the townsite work should be pushed under the present Commission to a speedy settlement, until the work is completed in the appraisement and sale of the townsites in the Choctaw and Chickasaw Nations, and that we hereby respectfully invite the attention of the Honorable Secretary of the Interior, to the utmost importance of an immediate completion of said work in order that the tribal affairs may be adjusted and a final settlement effected with the Government of the United States;

Be it further resolved. That a copy of this resolution be forwarded to the Honorable Secretary of the Interior, expressing this sentiment, and that this resolution shall take effect and be in force from and after its passage and approval.

Proposed by J. L Ward.

Approved this, the 28th day of October, 1904.

GREEN McCURTAIN,
P. C. C. N.

ATTEST:

J. W. CONSER,
Recording Secretary.

BILL NO. 15.

RESOLUTION ACCEPTING THE REPORT OF GEO. W. SCOTT, NATIONAL TREASURER, FOR THE FISCAL YEAR, BEGINNING OCT. 1ST, 1903, AND ENDING OCT. 1ST, 1904.

Your committee to whom was referred the report of Geo. W. Scott, National Treasurer, for the fiscal year beginning Oct. 1st. 1903, and ending Oct. 1st, 1904, have carefully examined said report and find that it shows receipts and disbursments as follows:

Total receipts, - -	$120,700.14
Total disbursments, - -	94,344.92
Balance on hand Oct. 1, 1904, -	$26,355.22

We, Therefore, recommend the adoption of the following resolution:

Be it Resolved by the General Council of the Choctaw Nation Assembled:

That the annual report of George W. Scott, National Treasurer, for the fiscal year, beginning Oct. 1, 1903, and ending Oct. 1, 1904, be and the same is hereby accepted as true and correct; and that this resolution shall take effect and be in force from and after its passage and approval.

Proposed by James Bower, Chairman of Finance Committee.

Approved this the 1st day of November, 1904.

GREEN McCURTAIN,
P. C. C. N.

ATTEST:

J. W. CONSER,
Recording Secretary.

BILL NO. 16.

RESOLUTION ACCEPTING THE REPORT OF GEORGE W. SCOTT, NATIONAL TREASURER RELATIVE TO HIS CONTINGENT FUND FOR THE FISCAL YEAR ENDED OCTOBER 1, 1904.

We, your Finance Committee, To whom was referred the report of Geo. W. Scott, National Treasurer, relative to his contingent fund for the fiscal year ended Oct. 1, 1904, of four hundred ($400) dollars of that office, beg leave to state, that we have carefully examined said report, and find the same to be a true and correct statement of the expenditure of said fund. Therefore we recommend the adoption of the following resolution:

Be it Resolved by the General Council of the Choctaw Nation Assembled:

That the report of Geo. W. Scott, National Treasurer, relative to the expenditure of the contingent fund of said office, be and the same is hereby accepted as true and correct, and this resolution shall take effect and be in force from and after its passage and approval.

Proposed by James Bower, Chairman of Finance Committee.

Approved this the 1st day of November, 1904.

GREEN McCURTAIN,
P. C. C. N.

ATTEST:

JOE W. CONSER,
Recording Secretary.

BILL NO. 17.

AN ACT APPROPRIATING THE SUM OF ONE THOUSAND ($1,000) DOLLARS, OR SO MUCH THEREOF AS MAY BE NECESSARY, TO DEFRAY THE EXPENSES OF LITIGATION, PROVIDED FOR THE CONTRACT WITH MESSRS. HILL AND BRIZZOLARA, COVERING THE SUIT OF THE CHOCTAW NATION AGAINST THE MISSOURI, KANSAS & TEXAS RAILWAY COMPANY.

Be it Enacted by the General Council of the Choctaw Nation Assembled:

SECTION 1. That the sum of one thousand ($1,000) dollars, or so much thereof as may be necessary, be and the same is hereby appropriated for the purpose of defraying the expenses to be incurred by Messrs. Hill and Brizzolara, as attorneys of the Choctaw Nation in its suit against the Missouri, Kansas & Texas Railway Company, as defined in the terms of the contract entered into between the Choctaw Nation, through its Principal Chief, and said Hill and Brizzolara; and the National Auditor is hereby directed, upon the certificates of the Principal Chief, to issue his warrants for that purpose, not exceeding in the aggregate the sum of one thousand ($1,000) dollars. and the National Treasurer is hereby authorized to pay the same out of any funds in the treasury not otherwise appropriated; and the contingent fund of the Principal Chief is hereby sufficiently increased to carry into effect the provisions of this act.

SEC. 2. That this act shall take effect and be in force from and after its passage and approval, and that all acts or parts of acts in conflict herewith are hereby repealed.

Proposed by James Bower, Chairman of Finance Committee.

Approved this the 1st day of Nov. 1904.

GREEN McCURTAIN,
P. C. C. N.

ATTEST:

J. W. CONSER,
Recording Secretary.

BILL NO. 18.

AN ACT FOR THE PAYMENT OF REGULAR EXPENSES NECESSARY TO PROTECT THE INTERESTS OF THE CHOCTAW NATION.

We, your committee, to whom has been referred the itemized accounts of Mansfield, McMurry & Cornish, for expenses incurred and legal services rendered, under the direction of the Principal Chief of the Choctaw Nation, in protecting its interest in the various matters that have arisen from Oct. 1, 1903, to September 30, 1904, have had the same under consideration, and after a careful investigation thereof, find the same to be true and correct. We have also had under consideration the matter of the necessity for making further provisions for the defense of Mississippi Choctaw citizenship cases and for handling patents. We therefore recommend the passage of the following bill:

Whereas, Regular and necessary expenses have been incurred and legal services have been rendered by Mansfield, McMurray & Cornish, under the direction of the Principal Chief of the Choctaw Nation, in protecting its interests, in various matters that have arisen from Oct. 1, 1903, to Sept. 30, 1904, and it is just and proper that provisions be made for the payment thereof, and also for the protection of the Choctaw Nation in various like matters that may hereafter arise from time to time; and,

Whereas, It is deemed of the highest importance that provision be made for the further defense of Mississippi Choctaw citizenship cases, pending before the Commission to the Five Civilized Tribes and the Department of the Interior until the same shall have been finally disposed of, and also that facilities be provided for the thorough and systematic conduct of the matter of the execution of patents and the delivery of the same to allotees in the Choctaw and Chickasaw Nations;

Therefore, Be it Enacted by the General Council of the Choctaw Nation Assembled:

SECTION 1. That the Principal Chief of the Choctaw Nation be, and he is hereby authorized, to direct the payment of such expenses as may have been incurred, not to exceed the sum of five thousand two hundred and eighty-two dollars and forty-six cents ($5,282.46), and such legal service as may have been rendered, not to exceed the sum of five thousand two hundred and fifty dollars ($5,250) by Mansfield, McMurray & Cornish, under his direction, in protecting the interest of the Choctaw Nation in various matters that have arisen from October 1, 1903, to September 30, 1904; payment therefore to be made in the following manner: Itemized accounts thereof shall be presented to the Principal Chief and upon his approval the National Auditor shall issue his warrant therefore. and the National Treasurer shall pay the same.

SEC. 2. The Principal Chief is further authorized to direct that such expenses be incurred, and such legal services rendered as in his judgment may be necessary to adequately protect the interests of the Choctaw Nation in the various matters that may hereafter arise from time to time. He is also authorized to direct the payment of such expenses as may be necessary to adequately defend Mississippi Choctaw citizenship cases, pending before the Commission to the Five Civilized

Tribes and the Department of the Interior; and also to handle in a thorough and systematic manner the matter of execution of patents and the delivery of the same to allottes in the Choctaw and Chickasaw Nations. Itemized accounts, of such expenses as may be so incurred, shall be presented to the Principal Chief, and upon his approval thereof, warrants shall be issued in payment thereof, and the National Treasurer shall pay the same.

SEC. 3. That the contingent fund of the Principal Chief, in addition to that now provided by law, is hereby increased sufficient to carry into effect the purposes of this act, and an appropriation therefor is hereby made; and that this act shall take effect and be in force from and after its passage and approval, and all acts or parts of acts in conflict herewith are hereby repealed.

Proposed by James Bower, Chairman of Finance Committee.

Approved this the 1st day of November, 1904.

GREEN McCURTAIN,
P. C. C. N.

ATTEST:
J. W. CONSER,
Recording Secretary.

BILL NO. 19.

AN ACT AMENDING THE LAW RELATIVE TO COUNTY AND PROBATE COURTS IN THE CHOCTAW NATION, AND REDUCING THE AMOUNT OF FUNDS HELD BY COUNTY TREASURERS FROM FIVE HUNDRED DOLLARS TO FIFTY DOLLARS.

Be it Enacted by the General Council of the Choctaw Nation Assembled:

SECTION 1. That hereafter the County Treasurer of each county in the Choctaw Nation, is hereby required to make full report to the National Treasurer of all funds received; and the act requiring each County Treasurer to retain five hundred ($500) dollars in said County Treasury, is so amended as to reduce said amount to fifty ($50) dollars.

SEC. 2. That all acts and parts of acts in conflict herewith are hereby repealed, and that this amended act shall take effect and be in force from and after its passage and approval.

Proposed by Daniel Webster, Chairman of Chief Message Committee.

Approved this the 1st day of November, 1904.

GREEN McCURTAN,
P. C. C. N.

ATTEST:

J. W. CONSER,
Recording Secretary.

BILL NO. 20.

We, your committee, to whom was referred the petition of Annie T. Arnote, (nee McCullie,) for compensation for services rendered the Choctaw Nation in teaching twenty (20) Choctaw children, under contract, at Antlers, I. T, for the period of five (5) months during the scholastic year of 1892 to 1893, would respectfully say that we have carefully examined said petition and find from oral and written testimony that the said Annie T. Arnote, (nee McCullie,) is entitled to the sum of one hundred and fifty ($150) dollars, and therefore recommend the passage of the following act:

Be it enacted by the General Council of the Choctaw Nation assembled:

SECTION 1. That the sum of one hundred and fifty ($150) dollars be and the same is hereby appropriated out of any money in the National Treasury not otherwise appropriated, to pay Mrs. Annie T. Arnote, (nee McCullie,) of Antlers, I. T., for services rendered in teaching Choctaw children during the scholastic year of 1892 to 1893:

SEC. 2. Be it further enacted: That the National Auditor is hereby authorized to issue his warrant and the National Treasurer to pay the same; and this act shall take effect and be in force from and after its passage and approval.

Proposed by James Bower, Chairman of Finance Committee.

Approved this the 1st day of November 1904.

GREEN McCURTAIN
P. C. C. N.

ATTEST:

J. W. CONSER,
Recording Secretary.

BILL NO. 21.

RESOLUTION ACCEPTING THE REPORT OF PETER J. HUDSON, NATIONAL AUDITOR.

We, your Finance Committee, to whom was referred the report of Peter J. Hudson, National Auditor, for the fiscal year ending September 30, 1904, have carefully examined same and find it true and correct, and therefore recommend the adoption of the following resolution:

Be it Resolved by the General Council of the Choctaw Nation Assembled.

SECTION 1. That the report of Peter J. Hudson, National Auditor, for the fiscal year ending September 30, 1904, be, and the same is hereby accepted as true and correct; and that this resolution shall take effect and be in force from and after its passage and approval.

Proposed by James Bower, Chairman of Finance Committee.

Approved this the 1st day of November, 1904.

GREEN McCURTAIN,

ATTEST: P. C. C. N.

JOE W. CONSER,

Recording Secretary.

BILL NO. 22.

COUNCIL HOUSE,
TUSHKAHOMA, IND. TER.,
October 31, 1904.

TO THEODORE ROOSEVELT, PRESIDENT OF THE UNITED STATES, WASHINGTON, D. C.

We, the people of the Choctaw Nation, through our representatives in National Council assembled, appeal to you with the full assurance that your personal familiarity with the conditions in the west will enable you to reach a just conclusion touching our welfare. It is appropriate in this condition to say, that we of the west do not hesitate to affirm that you, as President, more thoroughly represent western ideas than any former chief executive. We feel that we have in you a friend, and for that reason we speak with candor.

The people of the Choctaw Nation in their treaties with the United States government have ever contended for, and caused to be embodied in those agreements, a promise that no portions of their lands would ever be included in any state or territory without the full consent of the Five Civilized Tribes. This demand for, and promise of home rule, has been the strongest inducement held out to us as a people to gain our acquiescence and participation in the treaties made with the United States government. As a people, we have kept our faith with the United States government; have never violated the treaties entered into with it, and have lived in the belief that the undertakings of the United States with our people would be carried out in spirit and to the letter. Now as the time approaches for the consumation of the sacred pledge made to us, we are confronted with the disquieting fact that Congress is endeavoring to legislate to the detriment of the Five Civilized Tribes, and in contradiction of the solemn obligation imposed upon the United States government, under its treaties. Nor, have we as a people been silent. When the agitation was first inaugurated tending to violate the treaties made with us we voiced our opposition. We have addressed memorials to the United States Congress asking in the name of justice, in the name of honor, in the name of fair dealing, not to permit the passage of a law that would deprive us of our rights under the various solemn treaties made with the United States government, in whose honesty of purpose and integrity of motive we have ever believed. Our memorials have gone unheeded, and in the light of the confidence we have in you, our President, our cognizance of your interest in the welfare of your Indian citizens; your familiarity with our customs, and sympathy with our conditions, we come to you and request your intervention and assistance in bringing about the fulfillment of the promise by which the United States government secured the friendship of the Five Civilized Tribes; the consumation of the hope that has buoyed us; the light that has lead our footsteps along the path that must end in SEPERATE STATEHOOD.

There is now pending in the Senate of the United States a measure commonly known as the "Hamilton Bill," which has already passed the Lower House. This legislation has for its object the admission of Okla homa and the Indian Territory as one state. We desire now to emphatically reiterate our protest against the final enactment of this law. In the face of the pledge that has been made us; not once, but repeatedly, as is evidenced by the following extract from the various treaties made by the United States government with the Five Civilized Tribes:

"Whereas, It being the anxious desire of the Government of the United States to secure to the Cherokee Nation Indians a permanent home, and which shall under the most solemn guarantee of the United States, be and remain forever theirs, a home extended around it the lines, or placed over it, the jurisdiction of a Territory or a State, nor be pressed upon by the extension in any way of any of the limits of any existing Territory or State." (Treaty of 1828.)

"No Territory or State shall ever have the right to pass laws for the government of the Choctaw Nation of red men and their descendents; and no part of the land granted them shall ever be embraced in any Territory or State." (Treaty of 1830.)

"The United States hereby covenant and agree that the lands ceeded to the Cherokee Nation in the foregoing article shall in no future time, WITHOUT THEIR CONSENT, be included within the territorial limits or jurisdiction of any State or Territory." (Treaty of 1835.)

"The United States do hereby solemnly agree and bind themselves that no State or Territory shall ever pass laws for the government of the Creek and Siminole tribes of Indians, and that no portion of either of the tracts of country defined in the first and second articles of this agreement shall ever be embraced or included within or annexed to any Territory or State, nor shall either, or any part of either, ever be erected into a territory without the full and free consent of the legislative authority of the tribe owning the same." (Treaty of 1856.)

"This stipulation is made in the belief that the tribal government so modified will prove so satisfactory that there will be no need or desire for further change until the lands now occupied by the Five Civilized Tribes shall, in the opinion of Congress, be prepared for admission as a State to the Union.'. (Atoka agreement, ratified 1898.)

We are unalterably, determinedly, and for all time opposed to the amalgamation of Indian Territory and Oklahoma. We feel, and it is this thought that prompts us to address you, that your familarity with the language of the treaties solemnly executed between the United States government and the Five Civilized Tribes, will not countenance a prostitution of the sacred obligations of the United States. And the unfair attempt to pass a law that will abrogate the clause written in the agreements of the United States with the Five Civilized Tribes, that the lands of the Five Civilized Tribes would forever remain intact, would never be embraced in any State or Territory without the full consent of the Five Civilized Tribes, is a vicious effort to debase the honor of the United States government, and at the same time, deprive the Five Civilized tribes of the fruits of the pledge that moved them to execute their treaties with the United States government.

Knowing your intense honesty, your hatred of shams, and believing that your interest in our welfare is so deep rooted that you will thwart any measure aimed at our people, we appeal to you direct, asking you to take such steps as in your judgment will insure the carrying out of the pledge so sacredly and solemnly made to us, that the lands of the Five Civilized Tribes would never be included in any state or territory without the full consent of the Five Civilized Tribes. We are unalterably opposed to merging our lands with those of Oklahoma; we respectfully petition that justice be shown us, and that when Indian Territory is admitted to statehood that it will be allowed to enter the sisterhood of States, not as a part of Oklahoma, but as a soverign commonwealth, as was promised in the treaties made with us as a people; and as we have ever hoped for since first our forefathers affixed their signatures to the first treaty with the United States government.

We are fitted for statehood; we, together with our non-citizen brothers, are qualified for government of our own state; the population, area and resources of the Indian Territory are far in advance of many states of the Union, as will quickly appear from the following statistics:

In area the Indian Territory is twenty-nine times as large as Rhode Island, sixteen times as large as Deleware, six times as large as Connecticut, four times as large as New Jersey, almost four times as large as Massachusetts, three times as large as New Hampshire, three times as large as Vermont, three times as large as Maryland. It has six thousand square miles more than West Virginia, fifteen thousand square miles more than Maine, twelve hundred square miles more than South Carolina, is practically the size of Indiana, and is four-fifth the size of either Ohio, Kentucky, Virginia or Tennessee. The Choctaw Nation alone is larger than either Rhode Island, Delaware, Connecticut, New Jersey, Massachusetts, New Hampshire. Vermont or Maryland.

According to the census of 1900 the population of the Indian Territory was 392,060, which exceeded the population of seven States and five Territories, namely: Nine times that of Nevada, six times that of Alaska, four times that of Wyoming, three times that of Arizona, twice that of Hawaii, twice that of Deleware, twice that of Idaho, and twice that of New Mexico; it had a population of 148,000 more than Montana, 113,000 more than the District of Columbia, 115,000 more than Utah, and 72,000 more than North Dakota.

The population in 1900 was greater than that of Nevada, Idaho, Wyoming and Alaska combined. Since the last census emigration to the Indian Territory has been enormous, and it is safe to say that the present population exceeds that of either Oklahoma, Oregon, Rhode Island, South Dakota, Washington, Colorado, Florida, or New Hampshire.

In natural resources the Indian Territory is not unsurpassed by any state in the Union. Oil and natural gas has been developed in each of the Five Nations, but on the account of holdings of lands in common have not been operated. The same conditions obtains with reference to lead, zinc, iron and other minerals. The coal and asphalt deposits of the Indian Territory are superior to those of any State in the southwest. The coal industry is but in its infancy, and yet the annual report of the United States mine inspector for the year ended June 30, 1903, will show that during that year more than three million tons of coal were mined in the

Choctaw Nation alone.

In each of the other nations are extensive fields of coal, which are being rapidly developed and operated. In the Choctaw and Chickasaw Nations approximately 440,000 acres of coal and asphalt lands have been reserved from allotment. It has the most productive soil, four-fifths of which may be profitably farmed. Two-fifths have never been touched by the plow. Wheat, oats, corn and cotton, and most any product of the soil may be grown here.

In conclusion we turn to you, Mr. President, feeling that you will understand us better than Congress. As already stated, you know the west, you know our hopes and our ambitions, and we appeal again to your sense of justice and fair dealing, asking that you lend such assistance as in your power to frustrate the passage of the so-called "Hamilton Bill," and in its place recommend legislation that will insure to us the consummation of the sacred promise of the United States government; the harvesting of the hopes we have long cherished, fed on the belief that what has been pledged to us by the United States government would be fulfilled; give us but separate statehood for Indian Territory.

Proposed by Wm. H. Harrison.

Approved this the 1st day of November, 1904.

GREEN McCURTAIN,
P. C. C. N.

ATTEST:

J. W. CONSER,
Recording Secretary.

BILL NO. 23.

AN ACT ABOLISHING THE OFFICE OF BOARD OF HEALTH AND REPEALING THE LAW IN RELATION THERETO.

Be it Enacted by the General Council of the Choctaw Nation Assembled.

SECTION 1. That the office of Board of Health of the Choctaw Nation is hereby abolished, and the law creating said office is hereby repealed.

SEC. 2. That all acts and parts of acts in conflict herewith are hereby repealed, and this act shall take effect and be in force from and after its passage.

Proposed by Ed. McDaniel.

Approved this the 2d day of November, 1904.

GREEN McCURTAIN,
P. C. C. N.

ATTEST:

J. W. CONSER,
Recording Secretary.

BILL NO. 24.

Whereas, The incursion of sportsmen, hunters and trappers from surrounding states have well nigh destroyed the game and fish, once abounded in Choctaw Nation; and,

Whereas, No general law on this subject is possible, except through an act of Congress, which will prohibit the ruthless destruction of fish and game within the boundaries aforesaid.

Be it Resolved by the General Council of the Choctaw Nation Assembled:

SECTION 1. That the Congress of the United States be petitioned to pass some appropriate measure looking to the protection of game and fish in the Choctaw Nation.

SEC. 2. That the Choctaw delegate to Washington be authorized to present this resolution to the proper Congressional Committee and urge the adoption of some measure to that end.

SEC. 3. That this resolution take effect and be in force from and after its passage.

Proposed by Wm H. Harrison.

Approved this the 2d day of November, 1904.

GREEN McCURTAIN,
P. C. C. N.

ATTEST:

JOE W. CONSER,
Recording Secretary.

BILL NO. 25.

RESOLUTION ACCEPTING THE REPORT OF G. W. DUKES, GREEN M'CURTAIN AND GEORGE W. SCOTT, UNDER THE ACT OF CONGRESS, ENTITLED "AN ACT FOR THE RELIEF OF CERTAIN INDIGENT CHOCTAW AND CHICKASAW INDIANS IN THE INDIAN TERRITORY, AND FOR OTHER PURPOSES."—APPROVED APRIL 29, 1902.

Whereas, Under an act of Congress on April 29, 1902, twenty thousand ($20,000) dollars were set aside, of the Choctaw and Chickasaw fund, that had been placed to their credit in the United States Treasury, derived from the sale of town lots, under the act approved June 28, 1898, for the purpose of relieving certain indigent Choctaw and Chickasaws in the Indian Territory; and,

Whereas, Gilbert W. Dukes, Principal Chief of the Choctaw Nation; George W. Scott, Treasurer of the Choctaw Nation, and Green McCurtain, ex-Principal Chief of the Choctaw Nation, were constituted a commission with authority to investigate and determine what Choctaw citizens are destitute and in absolute need of help, and are further authorized to supply said destitute Choctaws with the food necessary for their maintenance; and,

Whereas, The said Gilbert W. Dukes, George W. Scott and Green McCurtain, as a Choctaw commission, have submitted a full report, showing that said funds have been distributed in accordance with the act of Congress aforesaid, and that their report herein is found to be full, true and correct.

Be it Therefore Resolved by the General Council of the Choctaw Nation Assembled.

SECTION 1. That the report of Gilbert W. Dukes, Principal Chief; George W. Scott, Treasurer of Choctaw Nation, and Green McCurtain, ex-Principal Chief of Choctaw Nation, comprising the Choctaw commission created under "Act of Congress," entitled "An act for the relief of certain indigent Choctaws and Chickasaw Indians in the Indian Territory, and for other purposes," (Approved April 29, 1902), be and the same is hereby accepted as true and correct; and that this resolution shall take effect and be in force from and after its passage and approval.

Proposed by James Bower, Chairman of Finance Committee.

Approved this the 2d day of November 1904.

GREEN McCURTAIN
P. C. C. N.

ATTEST:

J. W. CONSER,
Recording Secretary.

BILL NO. 26.

We, your Committee on Finance, to whom was referred a national warrant, issued to Silverman and Zimmerman, numbered 36F, for the sum of fifty-six dollars and thirty-one cents ($56.31) and dated September 6, 1900; after a careful investigation do find that the said warrant is null and void, for the reason that in the issuance of the same the National Auditor incorporated the sum of six dollars and thirty cents, Cedar county scrip, wrongfully; we, therefore, recommend the adoption of the following resolution:

Be it Resolved by the General Council of the Choctaw Nation Assembled:

SECTION 1. That the warrant heretofore issued for the sum of fifty-six dollars and thirty cents ($56.30), be declared null and void, and the Auditor is hereby required to issue in its place another warrant for the sum of fifty dollars ($50), payable to Silverman and Zimmerman, and that the National Treasurer shall pay the same out of any moneys in the treasury, not otherwise appropriated.

SEC. 2. That this resolution shall take effect and be in force from and after its passage and approval.

Proposed by James Bower, Chairman of Finance Committee.

Approved this the 2d day of November, 1904.

GREEN McCURTAN,

ATTEST: P. C. C. N.

J. W. CONSER,

Recording Secretary.

BILL NO. 27.

Be it Enacted by the General Council of the Choctaw Nation Assembled:

That the following sums of money are hereby appropriated out of the National Treasury, to defray the regular and necessary expenses of the government for the fiscal year commencing October 1, 1904, and ended September 30, 1905:

Principal Chief's salary - - - - -	$2,000 00
National Secretary's salary - - - - -	600 00
National Auditor's salary - - - - -	600 00
National Treasurer's salary - - - - -	600 00
National Attorney's salary - - - - -	400 00
Private Secretary's salary - - - -	1 000 00
Trustee coal and asphalt under Atoka agreem't	4,000 00

Nine national light horsemen - - - -	$1,400 00
Three Supreme Judges - - - - -	1,200 00
Three Circuit Judges - - - - - -	1,500 00
Seventeen County Judges - - - -	4,250 00
Three District Chiefs - - - - - -	150 00
Three District Attorneys - - - - -	1,500 00
Election Judges and Clerks - - - -	490 00
Grand and Petit Jurors - - - - -	3,525 00
Witnesses at Circuit Court - - - -	1,500 00
Contingent Fund for Principal Chief -	6,162 00
" " National Auditor -	600 00
" " " Treasurer -	400 00
" " " Secretary -	450 00
Sheriff and deputies attending Circuit Court	675 00
Publication fund, National Secretary - -	350 00
Clerk Supreme Court - - - - -	100 00
Three Circuit Clerks - - - - - -	900 00
Seventeen County Clerks - - - -	1,700 00
" " Sheriffs - - - - -	5,100 00
Thirty-four Deputy Sheriffs - - - -	3,400 00
Seventeen County Rangers - - - -	850 00
Caring for Capital Building - - - -	75 00
Delegate to Washington, D. C., salary - -	2,500 00
" " " expenses -	1,000 00
Supreme Judge's mileage - - - -	110 00
Act approved by the Principal Chief Oct. 19, 1899, and by the President of United States June 10, 1900 - - - - -	5,000 00
Act passed and approved by the Principal Chief Nov. 1, 1899, and approved by President McKinley December 8, 1899, - -	2,500 00
Expenses to carry on law suit of M. K. & T. R.	

R. Co. vs. Choctaw Nation - -	$1,000 00
Expense of attending funeral of Capt. J. S. Stanley - - - -	50 00
Light horsemen attending Council - -	987 00
Expenses of General Council, October 1904,	8,000 00

That this act shall take effect and be in force from and after its passage and approval.

Proposed by James Bower, Chairman of Finance Committee.

Approved this the 2d day of November, 1904.

GREEN McCURTAIN,

ATTEST: P. C. C. N.

J. W. CONSER,

Recording Secretary.

BILL NO. 28.

RESOLUTION THANKING HONORABLE GREEN M'CURTAIN, PRINCIPAL CHIEF.

Whereas, Human nature seems prone to speak kindly only of the dead; and,

Whereas, It seems appropriate to pay tribute to the living, in the person of our present chief executive, Honorable Green McCurtain; and,

Whereas, His long and honorable career in the public service of the Choctaw Nation entitles him to the gratitude of his people.

Be it Resolved by the General Council of the Choctaw Nation Assembled:

SECTION 1. That Hon. Green McCurtain, Principal Chief of the Choctaw Nation, be given a vote of thanks by Council for his untiring energy, his sincere zeal and never flagging purpose to secure to his people their property rights and an equal division thereof;

Be it further resolved, That Hon. Green McCurtain be presented with an engrossed copy of these resolutions as a manifestation of our esteem;

Be it further resolved, That these resolutions take effect and be in force from and after its passage.

Proposed by Frank Folsom.

Approved this the 2d day of November 1904.

GREEN McCURTAIN
P. C. C. N.

ATTEST:

J. W. CONSER,
Recording Secretary.

BILL NO. 29.

To the Hon. Eathan Allen Hitchcock, Secretary of the Interior, Washington, D. C.

Whereas, Under the terms of the supplimentary agreement, all citizens of the Choctaw and Chickasaw Nation who owned improvements situated on lands seg-gregated as coal lands, were to have the same appraised by a board of appraisers, under rules and regulations prescribed by the Honorable Secretary of the Interior; and,

Wheras, Said appraisers have refused to estimate and appraise cleared land on said segregated coal lands, giving as their reason therefor, that said appraisement of cleared land would be contrary to instructions; and,

Whereas, The failure of said appraisers to take into consideration the cost incurred by the citizen in clearing, breaking and putting in state of cultivation said land, and in many instances having reaped no benefits whatever from its use; and,

Whereas, The continued refusal and failure of the appraisers to consider the character of improvement will work untold hardship on the citizens who are largely dependent upon remuneration from this source, therefore;

Be it Resolved by the General Council of the Choctaw Nation Assembled:

SECTION 1. That the Honorable Secretary of the Interior be memoralized to instruct the appraisers to estimate the number of acres of cleared land owned by citizens on land segregated for coal purposes, and to allow said citizens reasonable compensation therefor: be it further resolved;

SEC. 2. That the delegate to Washington be authorized to present this memorial and urge favorable action on same, and that this resolution shall take effect and be in force from and after its passage and approval.

Proposed by Daniel Webster, Chairman of Chief Message Committee.

Approved this the 2d day of November, 1904.

GREEN McCURTAIN,
P. C. C. N.

ATTEST:

J. W. CONSER,
Recording Secretary.

BILL NO. 30.

To Theodore Roosevelt, President of the United States, Washington, D. C.

We, your memoralists, most through the accredited delegate of the Choctaw Nation at Washington, D. C., that the enactment of recent legislation of Congress touching probate matters, has brought many evils upon us instead of the intended good designed by Congress.

Under the law that now obtains, each parent is required to give bond for the management and care of his children's estate. This construction of the law gives a class of adventurers, known as "grafters," a wide field to put many nefarious schemes in operation, which are calculated to work a great injury to the Choctaw people, generally, and the ignorant full blood Indians in particular. The outrage practiced here by the "grafters" under the guise of law, is sickening in detail. The perjury and subordination of perjury that abounds would fill a volume.

One of the favorite methods of separating the Indian from his surplus lands, is for the "grafter" to induce the Indian to go to a border town, fill him up on mean whiskey, put a pint or two in his grip and then rush him back to the Indian Territory, where he is promptly arrested. The "grafter" is usually admitted to the bar of some Territory court and passes as an attorney. He then appears and offers bond for his incarcerated victim, and by this method completes his nefarious scheme. But the most profitable and less expensive method of securing the Indian's property, is by insisting that under the law they must apply to the United States Coutrs by petition for the appointment as guardian of their own children. By this insistence they have induced a large number of Indians to relinquish their rights in favor of the so-called "grafter." These practices by this class of adventurers have been widespread in the Choctaw and Chickasaw Nations, and unless some relief is offered these people by Congress the evils here enumerated will grow to immense proportions and lead to further outrages in the name of law.

We, therefore most respectfully request that in your message to Congress, that you point out the evil herein complained of, and suggest some appropriate remedy.

The authorized delegate of the Choctaw Nation has been directed to present this memorial, and to respectfully present further details of the deplorable situation here as a result of the legislation which Congress has thought appropriate to the conditions existing here.

And it is in the sense of the Choctaw Council, in general session assembled, that the delegate to Washington be instructed to present this memorial to the President, in person, and that this memorial shall take effect and be in force from and after its passage and approval by the Principal Chief.

Proposed by Silas Bacon.

Approved this the 2d day of November, 1904.

GREEN McCURTAIN,
P. C. C. N.

ATTEST:

JOE W. CONSER,
Recording Secretary.

THIS IS TO CERTIFY, That the above and foregoing is a full, true and correct copy of the Original Acts and Resolutions of the Choctaw General Council, passed at its Regular Session for the year 1904, the originals whereof are now on file in the office of the National Secretary of said Nation.

IN TESTIMONY WHEREOF, I Edward H. Wilson, National Secretary of said Nation, have hereunto affixed my official signature and the seal of the Choctaw Nation. Done this the 21st day of May, in the year one thousand nine hundred and five.

EDWARD H. WILSON,
National Sec., Choctaw Nation.

[SEAL.]

INDEX.

ACTS AND RESOLUTIONS OF THE GENERAL COUNCIL OF THE CHOCTAW NATION

Passed at its Extraordinary
and Regular Sessions, 1905

PART ONE

Acts Of The Choctaw Nation.

BILL NO. 1

AN ACT

TO RATIFY AN AGREEMENT BY AND BETWEEN THE ADJUSTING COMMISSION ON THE PART OF THE CHOCTAW NATION, AND A LIKE COMMISSION ON THE PART OF THE CHICKASAW NATION,

Whereas. The Commission created under an act of the General Council of the Choctaw Nation appointed on the 27th day of October, 1904, have made and concluded an agreement with a like Commission on the part of the Chickasaw Nation created under an Act of the Legislature of the Chickasaw Nation, approved on the 19th day of November, A. D., 1904; said agreement being in words and figures as follows, to-wit:

MEMORANDUM OF AGREEMENT

made and entered into on this, the 9th day of March, 1905, by and between the Commissioners on the part of the Choctaw Nation, and Commissioners on the part of the Chickasaw Nation, to adjust the differences heretofore existing between said Nations.

Whereas, The Choctaw Nation alléges and claims that the Chickasaw Nation is indebted to it in a sum unascertained for the cost of collection of the Chickasaw Nation's one-fourth interest in the Coal Royalties, which collections were made by the Choctaw Nation and turned over to the Chickasaw Nation up to the year 1888, or thereabout, and for which cost of collection of the Chickasaw Nation's one-fourth interest, the Choctaw Nation has never been re-imbursed; and,

Whereas, The Chickasaw Nation alleges and claims that the Choctaw Nation is indebted to it in an unascertained sum on account of royalties collected by the Choctaw Nation, one-fourth of which the said Chickasaw Nation claims; and,

Whereas, The Chickasaw Nation alleges and claims that the Choctaw Nation is indebted to it in the sum of seventeen thousand, twenty-five dollars and fifty cents ($17,025.50), that being one-fourth of the judgment of the Supreme Court of the United States (119 U. S. 306) confirming a like judgment of the Court of Claims wherein the Choctaw Nation was adjudged to be entitled to the sum of sixty-eight thousand, one hundred and two dollars ($68,102.00), from the Government of the United States on account of the land taken from the Choctaw Nation by the State of Arkansas, by reason of an inaccurate survey of the boundary line between the said State of Arkansas and the Choctaw Nation, made by the Government of the United States; and,

Whereas, Both said Nations have long disputed the claims against them respectively, but being willing and anxious to make an adjustment, such as would be fair and equitable, have, in an endeavor to obtain this end, appointed commissioners with authority to consider and agree upon all matters of difference existing between said Nations.

NOW, THEREFORE, BE IT AGREED AND RECOMMENDED BY THE COMMISSIONS TO THEIR RESPECTIVE NATIONS. —WITNESSETH:

FIRST—That the parties hereto have agreed and by these presents do agree that, in consideration of the common interest and mutual welfare of the Choctaw and Chickasaw Nations, that all detail matters of difference are hereby waived, and an adjustment shall be made upon a basis of a general settlement of any and all matters in dispute.

SECOND—The Choctaw Nation withdraws and forever abandons it's claim against the Chickasaw Nation for cost of collection of coal royalties collected by the Choctaw Nation and turned over to the Chickasaw Nation.

THIRD—The Chickasaw Nation withdraws and forever abandons it's claim against the Choctaw Nation for coal royalties alleged to have belonged to the Chickasaw Nation and collected by the Choctaw Nation.

FOURTH—The Choctaw Nation agrees to recognize and pay the claim of the Chickasaw Nation for one-fouth the money recieved on account of the eastern boundry question, decided in favor of the Choctaw Nation against the United States, as aforesaid, the said one-fourth amounting to seventeen thousand, twenty-five dollars and fifty cents ($17,025.50) and upon the Chickasaw Nation's accepting said amount in the manner herein after provided, less the costs, as provided herein, it shall forever abandon any and all claims aginst the said Choctaw Nation.

FIFTH—The Chickasaw Nation agrees to allow the Choctaw Nation a credit of one thousand, twenty-one dollars and fifty three cents ($1,021.53) as the Chickasaw Nation's pro rata share of the cost of the prosecution of the suit to recover the amount due by the Government in settlement of the eastern boundary dispute, aforesaid.

SIXTH—This agreement shall become binding upon the Choctaw and Chickasaw Nations when ratified and approved by the legislative authorities of the two Nations respectively.

WITNESS OUR HANDS AND SEALS, This the 9th day of March, 1905.

GREEN MCCURTAIN,	WM. H. MCMURRAY,
D. C. MCCURTAIN,	J. WES. PARKER,
S. B. SPRING,	DAVID FOLSOM,
Choctaw Commissioners.	Chickasaw Commissioners.

Whereas, Said agreement will settle forever the long standing differences between the two Nations, therefore,

BE IT ENACTED BY THE GENERAL COUNCIL OF THE CHOCTAW NATION IN EXTRAORDINARY SESSION ASSEMBLED

SEC. 1. That said agreement be and the same is hereby ratified and affirmed.

SEC. 2. That said Act take effect and be in force from and after its passage and approval and the ratification thereof by the legislature of the Chickasaw Nation and its approval thereof.

Recommended by ROBERT MORRIS.

Approved this the 30th day of June, 1905.

GREEN McCURTAIN,

P. C. C. N.

BILL NO. 2.

We, Your Finance Committee, to whom was referred the account of George W. Scott, with voucher attached, for $425.00, which sum was by him paid out, under the direction of the Principal Chief for repairs required on the Capitol building by reason of damages to such building by wind and rain during the month of April, 1905, beg to report that said account is for money actually expended by George W. Scott, and we therefore recommend the passage of the following Act:

BE IT ENACTED BY THE GENERAL COUNCIL OF THE CHOCTAW NATION IN EXTRAORDINARY SESSION ASSEMBLED

That the sum of Four Hundred and Twenty-Five Dollars, be, and the same is hereby appropriated out of any funds in the National Treasury, not otherwise appropriated for the payment of George W. Scott, and that the National Auditor be, and he is hereby authorized and directed to draw his National Warrant therefor.

And this Act shall take effect and be in force from and after its approval.

Proposed by FRANK FOLSOM, Chairman Finance Committee.

Approved this the 30th day of June, 1905.

GREEN McCURTAIN,

P. C. C. N.

BILL NO. 3.

AN ACT FOR THE RELIEF OF MATILDA HARRELL AND OTHERS.

Whereas, It appears after a thorough investigation, that Matilda Harrell and her children, Emily Harrell, Lemon Harrell and James Harrell, Choctaws by blood, were entitled to share in the distribution of what was known as the "Leased District" fund, and,

Whereas, For some reason they have not received their pro rata share, amounting to One Hundred and Three dollars ($103.00) each,

THEREFORE

Be it enacted by the General Council of the Choctaw Nation in Extraordinary Session Assembled:

SEC. 1. That the sum of Four Hundred and Twelve Dollars ($412.00) be, and the same is hereby appropriated out of any money in the National Treasury not otherwise appropriated to pay Matilda Harrell, Emily Harrell, Leon Harrell and James Harrell, their share for the Leased District fund.

SEC. 2. Be it further enacted that the National Auditor is hereby authorized to issue his Warrant, and the National Treasurer to pay the same, and this Act shall take effect and be in force from and after its passage and approval.

Proposed by ED. MCDANIEL.

Approved 30th day of June, 1905.

GREEN McCURTAIN,
P. C. C. N.

White House, Washington, D. C., Sept. 23, 1905.
Approved. THEODORE ROOSEVELT.

BILL NO. 4

A RESOLUTION AUTHORIZING THE NATIONAL AUDITOR TO ISSUE A DUPLICATE WARRANT NO. 54 D. IN PLACE OF THE ORIGINAL, LOST OR MISPLACED.

We, Your Finance Commitee, to whom was referred the petition of Will Everidge requesting Council to authorize the National Auditor to issue a duplicate warrant in the place of warrant No. 54 D, issued on Jan. 1 1905, in favor of Will Everidge which has been lost or misplaced so that it connot be found. After a thorough investigation we, your Finance Commitee, find that said warrant has been lost or misplaced and recommend the adoption of the following resolution.

Be it Resolved by the General Council of the Choctaw Nation in Extraordinary Session Assembled:

SEC. 1 That the National Auditor be authorized to issue a duplicate warrant in the sum of $25.25, Twenty-Five Dollars and Twenty-Five Cents to Will Everidge in place of Warrant No. 54 D, and that the National Treasurer shall pay same out of any fund not otherwise appropriated.

SEC. 2 That this resolution shall take effect and be in force from and after it's passage and approval.

Proposed by FRANK FOLSOM, Chairman Finance Committee.

Approved this July 3rd 1905.

GREEN McCURTAIN,
P. C. C. N.

BILL NO. 5.

AN ACT FAVORABLE TO VESTING AUTHORITY IN THE PRINCIPAL CHIEF OF THE CHOCTAW NATION TO MAKE FINAL DISPOSITION OF ALL TRIBAL AFFAIRS AFTER THE EXPIRATION OF THE CHOCTAW TRIBAL GOVERNMENT.

Whereas, The Atoka Agreement, among other things, provides that our Tribal Government "Shall Continue for a Period of Eight Years from the Fourth of March, Eighteen Hundred and Ninety-Eight:"

Whereas, There is no disposition on the part of the Choctaw Council to ask Congress for an extension of the Tribal Government by reason of the expense connected therewith; and

Whereas. It is apparent that many matters of vast importance to the Choctaw people, will not have been settled by the time set for the expiration of the Tribal Government, namely: The signing of Patents to Mississippi Choctaws, whose rights to such Patents will not have matured on March 4, 1906; the signing of Patents to Town Lots, for which the full amount will not have been paid on March 4, 1906, and Patents to land that will be in contest at the date of the expiration of the Tribal Government; the disposition of the surplus lands, and the Coal and Asphalt lands and Coal and Asphalt deposits, and the signing of Patents therefor, and such other rights as may arise in the settlement of the Tribal estate; and.

Whereas, It is right and proper that the Choctaw people should have some voice in the final settlement of their affairs after their Tribal Government shall have ceased,

Therefore, Be it Enacted by the General Council of the Choctaw Nation in Extraordinary Session Assembled:

SEC, 1. That it is the sense of the General Council that the Principal Chief should be constituted and empowered in behalf of the Choctaw Nation, with full authority generally, to do and perform all and every act requisite or proper to effectually wind up the Tribal affairs of the Choctaw Nation remainining unsettled at the expiration of the Tribal Government on March 4, 1906, to all intents and purposes, with the same validity as if the Tribal Government was acting with full authrity itself; and we, the General Council, hereby confirm all of the said aets of the Principal Chief as fully as if done by the Tribal Government.

SEC. 2. That this Act shall take effect on and after March 4, 1906.

Proposed by DANIEL WEBSTER, Chairman, Committee on Chief's Message.

Approved this the 3rd. day of July 1905.

GREEN McCURTAN,
P. C. C. N.

BILL NO. 6.

AN ACT IN RELATION TO THE SALE OF THE SEGREGATED COAL AND ASPHALT LANDS IN THE CHOCTAW AND CHICKASAW NATIONS.

Whereas, Coal and asphalt lands and coal and asphalt deposits in the Choctaw and Chickasaw Nations agregating not to exceed five hundred thousand acres, were segregated and provision made for the sale thereof at public auction under the provisions of sections fifty-eight and fifty-nine of the Act of Congress approved July 1, 1902, entitled:"An act to ratify and confirm an agreement with the Choctaw and Chickasaw Tribes of Indians and for other purposes," as follows:

"Within six months after the final ratification of this agreement the Secretary of the Interior shall ascertain so far as may be practicable, what lands are principally valueable because of their deposits of coal or asphalt, including therein all lands which at the time of the final ratification of this agreement shall be covered by then existing coal or asphalt leases, and within that time he shall by written order segregate and reserve from allotment all of said lands. Such segregation and reservation shall conform to the subdivisons of the Government survey as nearly as may be, and the total segregation and reservation shall not exceed five hundred thousand acres. No lands so reserved shall be allotted to any member or freedman, and the improvements of any member or freedman existing upon any of the lands so segregated and reserved at the time of their segregation and reservation, shall be appraised under the direction of the Secretary of the Interior, and shall be paid for out of any common funds of the two Tribes in the Treasury of the United States, upon the order of the Secretary of the Interior. All Coal and Asphalt deposits, as well as other minerals which may be found in any lands not so segregated and reserved shall be deemed a part of the land and shall pass to the allottee, or other person who may lawfully acquire title to such lands.

"All lands segregated and reserved under the last preceding Section, excepting those embraced within the limits of a Townsite, established as hereinbefore provided, shall, within three years from the final ratification of this agreement and before the disolution of the Tribal Governments, be sold at public auction for cash, under the direction of the President, by a Commission composed of three persons, which shall be appointed by the President, one on the recommendation of the Principal Chief of the Choctaw Nation, who shall be a Choctaw by blood, and one on the recommendation of the Governor of the Cnickasaw Nation, who shall be a Chickasaw by blood. Either of said commissioners may, at any time, be removed by the President for good cause shown. Each of said commissioners shall be paid at the rate of Four Thousand Dollars per annum, the Choctaw Commissioner to be paid by the Choctaw Nation, the Chickasaw Commissioner to be paid by the Chickasaw Nation, and the third Commissioner to be paid by the United States. In the sale of coal and asphalt lands and coal and asphalt deposits hereunder, the Commission shall have the right to reject any or all bids which it considers below the value of any such land or deposits. The proceeds arising from the sale of coal and asphalt lands and coal and asphalt deposits shall be deposited in the Treasury of the United States to the credit of said Tribes (freedmen excepted) with the other monies belonging to said Tribes in the manner provided by law. The lands embraced within any coal or asphalt lease shall be separately sold, subject to such lease, and the purchaser shall succeed to all the rights of the two Tribes of every kind and character, under the lease, but all advanced royalties received by the Tribes shall be retained by them. The lands so segregated and reserved, and not included within any existing coal or asphalt lease, shall be sold in tracts not exceeding in area a section under the Government survey;" and,

Whereas, By the Act of Congress, approved April 21, 1904, it was provided that such lands and such deposits should be sold, not at public auction as provided in the former act, but under the direction of the Secretary of the Interior, upon sealed proposals or bids, such provisions of law being as follows:

"All unleased lands which are by section fifty-nine of an act entitled "An Act to ratify and confirm an agreement with the Choctaw and Chickasaw tribes of Indians and for other purposes" approved July first nineteen hundred and two directed to be sold at public auction for cash, and all other unleased lands and deposits of like character in said nations segregated under any Act of Congress, shall, instead be sold under direction of the Secretary of the Interior in tracts not exceeding nine hundred and sixty acres to each person, after due advertisement, upon sealed proposals under regulations to be perscribed by the Secretary of the Interior and approved by the President with authority to reject any or all proposals: provided that the President shall appoint a commission of three persons, one on the recommendation of the Principal Chief of the Choctaw Nation, who shall be a Choctaw by blood, and one upon the recommendation of the Governor of the Chickasaw Nation who shall be a Chickasaw by blood, which commission shall have a right to be present at the time of the opening of bids and be heard in relation to the acceptance or rejection thereof.

All expenses' inclusive of necessary clerical help in the Department of the Interior, connected with and incident with such sale shall be paid from the funds of the Choctaw and Chickasaw tribes. on deposit in the Treasury of the United States: Provided, that all leased lands shall be held from sale until the further direction of Congress:" and,

Whereas, Notwithstanding the offering of such lands for sale, under sealed proposals or bids as provided in said Act, none have been sold, such proposals or bids thus made not having represented the fair value of the lands to which they applied; and such plan has, therefore proven a failure; and

Whereas: While it is realized that Congressional action is necessary to repeal existing law, and make effective any new plan of sale, yet it is proper that the initiative in the formation of a new plan should be taken by the Choctaws and Chickasaws, the intrested parties; and

Whereas, It is of the highest importance that such land should be sold and payment therefor made before the expiration of the Tribal Governments of the Choctaw and Chickasaw Nations to the end that our people may have a voice in the disposition of affairs of such vital importance to them,

Therefore, Be it enacted by the General Council of the Choctaw Nation in extraordinary session assembled (The Legislature of the Chickasaw Nation concurring,)

SEC. 1 That the Principal Chief of the Choctaw Nation be and he is hereby empowered and directed to take necessary steps on the part of the Choctaw Nation, the Chickasaw Nation concurring, to bring about the sale of coal and asphalt lands, and coal and asphalt deposits in the Choctaw and Chickasaw Nations segregated as above set out, for the highest price obtainable, either to private purchasers or to the government of the United States; and to that end he is hereby empowered to employ counsel or appoint commissioners to represent the Choctaw Nation in all matters connected therewith and agree, on behalf of the Choctaw Nation, that the council or commission so employed or appointed shall be paid as compensation for their services not to exceed 10 per centum of the sum which may be received from the lands and deposits sold, such compensation to be wholly contingent upon a sale being effected and payable wholly out of the monies received therefrom.

SEC. 2. That this Act shall take effect and be in force from and after its passage and approval.

Proposed by DANIEL WEBSTER, Chairman Committee on Chief's Message.

Approved this the 3rd. day of July 1905.

GREEN McCURTAN,
P. C. C. N.

BILL NO. 7.

BE IT ENACTED BY THE GRNERAL COUNCIL OF THE CHOCTAW NATION IN EXTRAORDINARY SESSION ASSEMBLED

That the sum of Twenty-Seven Hundred Dollars ($2,700.00), or so much as may be necessary, be and the same is hereby appropriated out of any monies in the National Treasury not otherwise appropriated to defray the expenses of the Choctaw National Council, in Extraordinary Session Assembled, which said extraordinary session was by Proclamation of the Principal Chief, convened on June 27, 1905.

tion the [illegible] to bring about the sale of coal and [illegible] coal and asphalt deposits in the Choctaw and [illegible] Nations segregated as above set out, for the highest price obtainable, either to private purchasers or to the government of the United States, and to that end he is hereby empowered to employ counsel or appoint commissioners to represent the Choctaw Nation in all matters connected therewith and agree, on behalf of the Choctaw Nation, that the council or commission so employed or appointed shall be paid as compensation for their services not to exceed [illegible] per centum of the sum which may be received from the lands and deposits sold, such compensation to be wholly contingent upon a sale being effected and payable wholly out of the monies received therefrom.

SEC. 2. That this Act shall take effect and be in force from and after its passage and approval.

Proposed by DANIEL WEBSTER, Chairman Committee on Chief's Message.

Approved this the [illegible] day of July 1905.

GREEN McCURTAIN,

P. C. C. N.

BILL NO. 7.

BE IT ENACTED BY THE GENERAL COUNCIL OF THE CHOCTAW NATION IN EXTRAORDINARY SESSION ASSEMBLED:

That the sum of Twenty Seven Hundred Dollars ($2,700.00), or so much as may be necessary, be and the same is hereby appropriated out of any monies in the National Treasury not otherwise appropriated to defray the expenses of the Choctaw Council in Extraordinary Session Assembled, which extraordinary session was by Proclamation [illegible] 1905.

(Reproduced as originally printed.)

herewith are hereby repealed, and this act shall take effect and be of full force from and after its passage and approval.

Proposed by DANIEL WEBSTER, Chairman Committee on Chief's Message.

Approved this the 3rd. day of July 1905.

GREEN McCURTAIN.
P. C. C. N.

BILL NO. 9.

RESOLUTION

RESOLUTION OF ADJOURNMENT.

BE IT RESOLVED BY THE GENERAL COUNCIL OF THE CHOCTAW NATION IN EXTRAORDINARY SESSION ASSEMBLED.

That the present session of Council do adjour July, 4, 1905. at ten o'clock A. M,

And this resolution shall take effect and be in force from and ofter it's passage.

Proposed by DAVIS GARLAND.

Approved this the 4th day of October, 1905.

GREEN McCURTAIN,
P. C. C. N.

PART TWO

Acts Of The Choctaw Nation.

BILL NO. 1.

Be it resolved by the General Council of the Choctaw Nation in regular session assembled:

SEC. 1. That the Chairman of the Finance Committee shall appoint a clerk for said committee, whose duty it shall be to make and keep a full record of the work of said committee.

SEC. 2. Be it further resolved, That the clerk of said committee shall receive for his services five dollars ($5) per day, that the National Auditor shall issue warrant for actual services, and the National Treasurer shall pay the same.

And this resolution shall take effect and be in force from and after its passage and approval.

E. A. MOORE.

Approved this the 4th day of October, 1905.

GREEN McCURTAIN,
P. C. C. N.

BILL NO. 2.

Be it resolved by the General Council of the Choctaw Nation in regular session assembled:

SEC. 1. That the Chairman of the Committee of Chief's Message, shall appoint a clerk of said committee, whose duty it shall be to make and keep a full record of the said committee.

SEC. 2. Be it further resolved, That the clerk of said committee of Chief's Message shall receive for his services the sum of four dollars ($4) per day, that the National Auditor shall issue his warrant for actual services, and the National Treasurer shall pay the same.

And this resolution shall take effect and be in force from and after its passage and approval.

Proposed by W. A. DURANT.

Approved this the 4th day of October, 1905.

GREEN McCURTAIN,
P. C. C. N.

BILL NO. 3.

Be it resolved by the General Council of the Choctaw Nation assembled:

SEC. 1. That the Chairman of the Committee on Petitions shall appoint a clerk for the said committee, whose duty it shall be to make and keep a full record of the work of said committee.

SEC. 2. Be it further resolved, That the clerk of said committee receive for his services four dollars ($4) per day, that the National Auditor shall issue warrant for actual services, and the National Treasurer shall pay the same.

And this resolution shall take effect and be in force from and after its passage and approval.

Proposed by SIMON TAYLOR.

Approved this the 4th day of October, 1905.

GREEN McCURTAIN,
P. C. C. N.

BILL NO. 4.

RESOLUTION

REQUIRING THE OFFICERS OF CEDAR, EAGLE, NASHOBA, BOKTUKLO AND KIAMITIA COUNTIES TO SUBMIT THEIR RECORDS FOR THE INSPECTION OF THE JUDICIARY COMMITTEE:

Whereas, In view of the approach and end of the Tribal Government, renders it necessary that steps be taken to examine the financial condition of those counties which are known to be in debt; and

Whereas, The Nation must assume such obligations as remain outstanding at the close of Tribal Government; and

Whereas, This authority is vested solely in the General Council of the Choctaw Nation:

THEREFORE

Be it resolved by the General Council of the Choctaw Nation assembled, That the Judiciary Committee is fully empowered with the aid of the Principal Chief to notify the officers of Cedar, Eagle, Nashoba, Boktuklo and Kiamitia counties, to appear before said Judiciary Committee, with the records of their respective counties, for the purpose of answering such questions relative to the financial condition of their respective counties, as may be propounded by the said Judiciary Committee.

Be it further resolved, That it shall be the duty of the Principal Chief to notify said officers to appear before said committee not later than 25th day of October, 905, and that this resolution shall take effect and be in force from and after its passage and approval.

Proposed by W. A. DURANT.

Approved this the 4th day of October, 1905.

GREEN McCURTAIN,
P. C. C. N.

BILL NO 5.

RESOLUTION OF ADJOURNMENT.

IN RESPECT TO THE MEMORY OF CHIEF JUSTICE JOSEPH GARLAND, DECEASED:

Whereas, The sad news has been communicated to us through our Chief Executive, of the sudden demise of Joseph Garland, Chief Justice of the Supreme Court of the Choctaw Nation, and

Whereas. His long and useful career has been of inestimable benefit to his people; and

Whereas. The purity of his character in his domestic relations and the integrity of his conduct as a judicial officer entitles his memory to our most profound respect.

THEREFORE

Be it resolved by the General Council of the Choctaw Nation assembled:

That in respect to the memory of this distinguished citizen, and steadfast friend; that the Senate and House of Representatives of the Choctaw Nation, in General Council assembled adjourn at 11 o'clock a. m,, this the 4th day of October 1905, and remain dissolved until Monday, October 9, 1905 at 9 o'clock a. m., and that the Principal Chief be directed to appoint a committee to attend the funeral of Chief Justice Garland; and

Be it further resolved, That the said committee so appointed carry to the members of Chief Justice Garland's family the sincere condolence of the Choctaw Council, in their hour of sad bereavement.

Proposed by DANIEL WEBSTER.

Approved this the 4th day of October, 1905.

GREEN McCURTAIN,
P. C. C. N.

BILL NO. 6.

RESOLUTION.

BE IT ENACTED BY THE GENERAL COUNCIL OF THE CHOCTAW NATION ASSEMBLED.

That the articles of impeachment against Solomon J. Homer, read, interpreted, passed the House of Representatives and referred to the Senate on th e 17th day of October, 1902; and the judgment of the Senate, rendered upon default on the 21st day of October, 1902, sitting as a Court of Impeachment, impeaching the said Solomon J. Homer, is hereby repealed and held for naught, and the said Articles of Impeachment and Judgment of the Senate are ordered to be expunged from the records of the General Council of the Choctaw Nation, by the National Secretary of the Choctaw Nation.

Proposed by J. L. WARD.

Approved this the 24th day of October, 1905.

GREEN McCURT AIN
P. C. C. N.

BILL NO. 7.

RESOLUTION.

APPOINTING A COMMITEE TO ATTEND SEPARATE STATEHOOD MEETING AT SOUTH MCALESTER ON OCTOBER 13, 1905.

Whereas, The advocates of Separate Statehood will assemble at South McAlester Indian Territory on Saturday October 14, 1905; and,

Whereas, The interest of the Indian will be largely subserved in our judgement through the success of the separate statehood plan.

THEREFORE

BE IT RESOLVED BY THE GENERAL COUNCIL OF THE CHOCTAW NATION ASSEMBLED.

That the Principal Chief is hereby authorized to name a Commitee composed of two members of the Senate and three members from the House of Represenatives who shall attend said meeting and who shall convey to that body so far as it may the well wishes and God-speed of the Choctaw people; and that this resolution shall take effect and be in force from and after it's passage and approval.

Proposed by ROBERT MORRIS.

Approved this the 12th day of October, 1905.

GREEN McCURTAIN,
P. C. C. N.

BILL NO. 8

RESOLUTION.

ENDORSING HON. JAMES E. GRESHEM FOR UNITED STATES DISTRICT ATTORNEY FOR THE CENTRAL DISTRICT OF THE INDIAN TERRITORY, AND REQUESTING HIS APPOINTMENT.

Whereas. Hon. James E. Gresham is applicant for the position of United States District Attorney for the Central District of the Indian Territory; and,

Whereas, His long and faithful service as Assistant District Attorney, entitles him to promotion; and,

Whereas, His uniform kindness in the enforcement of the law and his unflagging zeal in his effort to protect our timber against depredators has endeared him to the Choctaw people.

THEREFORE

BE IT RESOLVED BY THE GENERAL COUNCIL OF THE CHOCTAW NATION ASSEMBLED.

That the candidacy of Hon. James E. Gresham, for United States District Attorney for the Central District of the Indian Territory is hereby endorsed by the General Council of the Choctaw Nation, and that the President of the United States be respectfully reqested to appoint him, in recognition of his faithful service and strict enforcement of the law.

That an engrossed copy of this resolution be forwarded to the President of the United States conveying the sense of this body, and that this resolution take effect and be in force from and after its passage and approval.

Proposed by S. W. MAYTUBBY.

Approved this the 24th day of October, 1905.

GREEN McCURTAIN,
P. C. C. N.

BILL NO. 9.

RESOLUTION.

ENDORSING THE ACTION OF THE PRINCIPAL CHIEF RELATIVE TO THE CONSTITUTIONAL CONVENTION, AND IN RELATION THERETO.

Whereas: The Principal Chief of the Choctaw Nation, acting in conjunction with the Governors of the Cherokee, Creek, Chickasaw and Seminole Nations, called a constitutional convention at Muskogee, Indian Territory; and,

Whereas: Said convention was composed of the most representative and intelligent class of the inhabitants residing in the boundaries of the five civilized tribes; and,

Whereas: That convention has adopted and promulgated a constitution to be submitted to a vote of the people on Tuesday, November 7, 1905, that reflects the highest order of intelligence and patriotism on the part of the members composing that distinguished assembly; and,

Whereas: The treaties between the United States Government and the Five Civilized Tribes contain numerous provisions virtually pledging to the Indians thereof the creation of a state out of the Indian Territory independent and alone; and,

Whereas: The racial pride not yet extinct among our people craves the boon of one modest Indian State out of a domain which at one time almost composed the continent: and,

Whereas, In resources and material well-being the Indian Territory is equipped in every particular for statehood of and by itself.

THEREFORE

BE IT RESOLVED BY THE GENERAL COUNCIL OF THE CHOCTAW NATION ASSEMBLED.

Sec. 1. That the action of our Chief in his earnest efforts to secure statehood for the Indian Territory is hereby commended and endorsed.

Sec. 2. That the Constitution adopted by the said Constitutional Convention is hereby approved, and ratified by the General Council of the Choctaw Nation, because it more truly represents and reflects the sentiment and feeling of the great mass of people inhabiting the Indian Territory than any other published expression extant.

Sec. 3. That a copy of this resolution be forwarded to the President of the U nited States, conveying the sense of this body; and that this resolution shall take effect and be in force from and after its passage and approval.

Proposed by DANIEL WEBSTER, Chairman Committee on Chief's Message.

Approved this the 24th day of October, 1905.

GREEN McCURTAIN,
P. C. C. N.

BILL NO. 10.

RESOLUTION

ACCEPTING REPORT OF I. S. LOWERY, COLLECTOR FOR THE FIRST DISTRICT. C. N. FOR QUARTERS ENDED JUNE 30, 1905.

Your Committee to whom was referred the report of I. S. Lowery, district collector for the First District of the Choctaw Nation, have carefully examined the said report in detail, and find that it covers the following quarters to-wit:

Quarter ending	Sept. 30, 1904 - -	$ 725.00
" "	Dec. 31, 1904 - -	900.00
" "	March 31, 1905 - -	1012.15
" "	June 30, 1905 - -	14168.42
	Grand Total - - - -	$16805.57
	Less ten per cent - - -	1680.55
	Amount due Nation - -	$15125.01

The total amount due the Nation is shown to be sum of fifteen thousand one hundred and twenty-five dollars and one cent, ($15125.01.) Receipt from the National Treasurer shows that this amount has been paid in, and your committee recommend the adoption of the following resolution:

BE IT RESOLVED BY THE GENERAL COUNCIL OF THE CHOCTAW NATION ASSEMBLED.

That the report of I. S. Lowery, Collector for the

First District of the Choctaw Nation be and the same is hereby accepted as true and correct, and this resolution take effect and be in force from and after its passage and approval.

FRANK FOLSOM, Chairman Finance Committee.

Approved this the 24th day of October, 1905.

GREEN McCURTAIN,
P. C. C. N.

BILL NO. 11.

RESOLUTION.

ACCEPTING THE REPORT OF H. L. SANGUIN, COLLECTOR FOR THE THIRD DISTRICT OF THE CHOCTAW NATION, FOR THE QUARTERS ENDED JUNE 30, 1905.

Your Committee to whom was referred the report of H. L. Sanguin, District Collector for the Third District of the Choctaw Nation, have carefully examined the said reports in detail and find that it covers the following quarters to-wit:

Quarter ended Sept. 30, 1904,	- -	$ 772.70
" " Dec. 31, 1904,	- -	791.65
" " Mar. 31, 1905,	- -	80[illegible].25
" " June 30, 1905,	- -	12,658.77
Total	- - -	15028.37
Less ten per cent	- -	1502.83
		$13.525.54

The total amount due the Nation is shown to be the sum of thirteen thousand five hundred and twenty-five dollars and fifty-four cents ($13,525.54). Receipt from the national treasurer shows that this amount has been paid in and your Committee recommended the adoption of the following resoultion:

Be it resolved by the General Council of the Choctaw Nation Assembled.

That the report of H. L. Sanguin, Collector for the Third District of the Choctaw Nation be and the same is hereby accepted as true and correct, and this resolution shall take effect and be in force from and after its passage and approval.

FRANK FOLSOM, Chairman Finance Committee.

Approved this the 24th day of October, 1905.

GREEN McCURTAIN,
P. C. C. N.

BILL NO. 12.

AN ACT

TO DEFRAY THE EXPENSES OF THE COMMITTEE APPOINTED TO ATTEND THE SEPARATE STATEHOOD MEETING AT SO. MCALESTER, I. T., OCT. 13, 1905.

BE IT ENACTED BY THE GENERAL COUNCIL OF THE CHOCTAW NATION ASSEMBLED.

That the sum of $54.75 be and the same is hereby appropriated for the purpose of defraying the expenses of the Committee appointed to attend the Separate Statehood meeting at South McAlester, I. T., Oct, 13, 1905, and the National Auditor is hereby authorized to issue his warrants for the same as follows:

S. W. Maytubby - - - -	$10.95
Frank Folsom - - - - -	10.95
G. W. Choate - - - - -	10.95
S. Wilson - - - - -	10.95
Simon Taylor - - - - -	10.95
	$54.75

and the National Treasurer shall pay the same out of of any funds not otherwise appropriated; and this act shall take effect and be in force from and after its passage and approval.

Proposed by J. L. WARD.

Approved this the 24th day of October, 1905.

GREEN McCURTAIN,
P. C. C. N.

BILL NO. 13.

AN ACT

TO DEFRAY THE EXPENSES OF THE COMMITTEE APPOINTED TO ATTEND THE FUNERAL OF JUDGE GARLAND.

BE IT ENACTED BY THE GENERAL COUNCIL OF THE CHOCTAW NATION ASSEMBLED.

That the sum of $70.60 be and the same is hereby appropriated for the purpose of defraying the expenses of the committee appointed to attend the funeral of Judge Garland; and the National Auditor is hereby authorized to issue his warrants for the same as follows:

G. W. Choate	$11.10
Joe Ward	11,10
Frank Folsom	11.10
Joe Dukes	11.10
Turner Everidge	11.10
Ed McDaniel	8.75
John McBrayer	6.35
Total	$70.60

And the National Treasurer shall pay the same out of any funds not otherwise appropriated; and this act shall take effect and be in force from and after its passage and approval.

Proposed by FRANK FOLSOM.

Approved this the 24th day of October, 1905.

GREEN McCURTAIN,
P. C. C. N.

BILL NO. 14

AN ACT.

EMPOWERING THE DISTRICT JUDGES TO SELECT AND EMPANNEL JURORS.

BE IT ENACTED BY THE GENERAL COUNCIL OF THE CHOCTAW NATION ASSEMBLED.

Sec. 1. That the District Judges of the Choctaw Nation are hereby authorized and empowed to select jurors for their respective courts where County Judges have failed to comply with the law in this respect.

Sec. 2. That the said Judges shall have such discretionary power in the final disposition of the business pending in their respective courts as will enable them to clear the dockets.

Sec. 3. That all laws in conflict herewith are hereby repealed and this Act shall take effect and be in force from and after its passage and approval.

Proposed by J. L. WARD.

Approved this the 24th day of October, 1905.

GREEN McCURTAIN,
P. C. C. N.

BILL NO. 15.

RESOLUTION.

BE IT RESOLVED BY THE GENERAL COUNCIL OF THE CHOCTAW NATION ASSEMBLED.

That this Council take a recess until November 14, 1905; and that this resolution take effect andbe in force from and after Saturday at 10 o'clock a. m. October 28, 1905.

Proposed by FRANK FOLSOM.

Approved this the 24th day of October, 1905.

GREEN McCURTAIN,
P. C. C. N.

BILL NO. 16.

RESOLUTION.

AUTHORIZING THE PRINCIPAL CHIEF TO TAKE LEGAL STEPS TO RECOVER THE VALUE OF TIMBER UNLAWFULLY CUT FROM PUBLIC DOMAIN OF THE CHOCTAW NATION.

Whereas: Many million feet of pine timber has been cut from the domain of the Choctaw Nation by non-citizens, over the protest of the tribal government; and,

Whereas: The United States Government, through its intercourse laws and treaties solemnly guaranteed protection to our property interests; and,

Whereas: The United States Government, having failed to enforce the laws and treaties, has rendered itself liable to the Choctaw Nation.

THEREFORE

BE IT RESOLVED BY THE GENERAL COUNCIL OF THE CHOCTAW NATION ASSEMBLED.

Sec. 1. That the Principal Chief of the Choctaw Nation is hereby authorized to take the necessary steps to ascertain the amount of timber unlawfully cut from the public domain of the Choctaw Nation, and is hereby further authorized to take such legal action as he may deem necessary to recover the value of said timber from the United States Government.

Sec. 2. That this resolution shall take effect and be in force from and after its passage and approval.

Proposed by DANIEL WEBSTER, Chairman Committee on Chief's Message.

Approved this the 26th day of October, 1905.

GREEN McCURTAIN,

P. C. C. N.

BILL NO. 17.

RESOLUTION.

EMPOWERING THE PRINCIPAL CHIEF TO TAKE PROPER ACTION RELATIVE TO THE RE-ESTABLISHMENT OF THE BOUNDARY LINE BETWEEN THE CHOCTAW NATION AND THE STATE OF TEXAS.

Whereas, The original boundary line between the ChoctawNation and the state of Texas was plainly outlined by Red River; and,

Whereas, Said stream has shifted its current to such an extent as to cut off from the public domain of the Choctaw Nation many thousand acres of valuable land belonging to the Choctaw and Chickasaw Nations; and

Whereas, It is necessary to re-establish the orginal boundary line in order that we may intelligently dispose of these lands by allotment and otherwise.

THEREFORE

BE IT RESOLVED BY THE GENERAL COUNCIL OF THE CHOCTAW NATION ASSEMBLED.

Sec 1. That the Principal Chief of the Choctaw Nation is hereby authorized and empowered to take such action as may be necessary to re-established the boundary line between the Choc taw Nation and the state of Texas.

Sec. 2. Be it further resolved that the Principal Chief is hereby authorized to take such steps as deemed necessary to secure peacible possession of said lands and that this resolution shall take effect and be in force from and after its passage and approval.

Proposed by DANIEL WEBSTER, Chairman Committee on Chief's Message.

Approved this the 26th day of October, 1905.

GREEN McCURTAIN

P. C. C. N.

BILL NO. 18.

We, your Finance Committee, to whom was referred the account of T. D. Hibben, Supreme Clerk of the Choctaw Nation for twenty-five dollars ($25) for expenses incured by him in furnishing stationery for the office, and the keeping of the books, papers and seal for the last three years, would respectfully say that we have carefully examined said account and find that said T. D. Hibben is entitled to the sum of twenty-five dollars ($25), and therefore recommend the passage of the following Act:

BE IT ENACTED BY THE GENERAL COUNCIL OF THE CHOCTAW NATION ASSEMBLED.

Sec. 1. That the sum of twenty-five dollars ($25) be and the same is hereby appropriated out of any money in the National Treasury not otherwise appropriated, to pay T. D. Hibben for expenses incurred in furnishing stationery for the office, and the safe keeping of the books, papers and seal for the last three years.

Be it further enacted: That the National Auditor is hereby authorized to issue his warrant and the National Treasurer to pay the same; and this act shall take effect and be in force from and after its passage and approval.

Proposed by FRANK FOLSOM, Chairman Finance Committee.

Approved this the 30th day of October, 1905.

GREEN McCURTAIN,

P. C. C. N.

BILL NO. 19.

RESOLUTION.

ACCEPTING THE REPORT OF GEO. W. SCOTT, NATIONAL TREASURER, RELATIAE TO HIS CONTINGENT FUND FOR THE FISCAL YEAR ENDED OCTOBER, 1, 1905.

We, your Finance Committee, to whom was referred the report of Geo. W. Scott, National Treasurer, relative to the contingent fund for the fiscal year ending October 1st, 1905, of Four Hundred ($400.) Dollars of that office, beg leave to state, that we have carefully examined said report, and find the same to be a true and correct statement of the expenditures of said fund:

Therefore we recommend the adoption of the following resolution:

BE IT RESOLVED BY THE GENERAL COUNCIL OF THE CHOCTAW NATION ASSEMBLED:

That the report of Geo. W. Scott, National Treasurer, relative to the expenditure of the contingent fund of said office, be and the same is hereby accepted as true and correct, and this resolution shall take effect and be in force from and after its passage and approval.

Proposed by FRANK FOLSOM, Chairman of Finance Committee.

Approved this the 30th day of October, 1905.

GREEN McCURTAIN,
P. C. C. N.

BILL NO. 20.

RESOLUTION

ACCEPTING THE REPORT OF MCCURTAIN AND HILL, PROBATE ATTORNEYS FOR THE CHOCTAW NATION.

We, the Finance Committee, to whom was referred the report of McCurtain & Hill, Probate Attorneys for the Choctaw Nation beg leave to report that we have examined the annual report filed by said Attorneys and that we find their said report in all things true and correct, and in full and exact compliance with the law authorizing their employment. We therefore recommend the adoption of the following resolutions:

BE IT RESOLVED BY THE GENERAL COUNCIL OF THE CHOCTAW NATION ASSEMBLED.

That the report of McCurtain & Hill as Probate Attorneys for the Chootaw Nation be and the same is hereby accepted as true and correct; that this resolution take effect from and after its passage and approval.

Proposed by FRANK FOLSOM, Chairman Finance Committee.

Approved this the 30th day of October, 1905.

GREEN McCURTAIN,
P. C. C. N.

BILL NO, 21.

MEMORIAL

RESPECTFULLY REQUESTING THE DEPARTMENT OF THE INTERIOR TO ORDER THE PAYMENT OF FUNDS BELONGING TO CERTAIN ALLOTTEES AND OTHER PURPOSES.

Whereas: Under the rules and regulations of the Interior Department the value of the timber cut from individual allotments by railway corporations was payable to the United States Indian Agent to be placed to the credit of the individual allottee; and

Whereas: Said payments have been made in full by said railway corporations; and

Whereas: Said funds are due and payable to the individual allottees, since the completion of their allotments.

THEREFORE

BE IT RESOLVED BY THE GENERAL COUNCIL OF THE CHOCTAW NATION ASSEMBLED.

Sec. 1. That the Honorable Secretary of the Interior be respectfully requested to order said funds paid over to such allottees as may be entitled to participate in the distri bution thereof, and that this resolution take effect and be in force from and after its passage and approval.

Proposed by DANIEL WEBSTER, Chairman Committee on Chief's Message.

Approved this the 30th day of October, 1905.

GREEN McCURTAIN
P. C. C. N.

BILL NO. 22.

AN ACT

FOR THE RELIEF OF CLYDAS HARVEY.

United States of America,
Central District,
Indian, Territory.

Be it remembered, that

Before me W. H. McKinney, a Notary Public within the said district and Territory, personally appeared Green Harvey, who being duly sworn according to law and oath state that he is a citizen by blood of the Choctaw Nation, that his post office address is Damon, I. T., and further makes the following statement: "I am 42 years of age, that I am own father of a child by the name of Glottis who was born on the 20th day of July, 1893 and who is now living. Her own mother, my legal wife Ellen Harvey died February 17th, 1897 at Damon I. T." And further states that, "I did not get the money for my child, Clydas Harvey, from the Leased District money which was paid to the citizens of the Choctaw Nation. I was instructed by Hon. Green McCurtain, who was Treasurer of the Choctaw Nation at that time, that the affidavit should be made first showing the date of birth of the said child, Glottis, and then

I was to get the money for the child, but when the payment was over, I thought I would not get any money, and never applied to the proper authority. But lately I was informed that if I make a petition to the Council I could get the money which is justly entitled to my child."

Green Harvey.

Subscribed and sworn to before me this 26th day of October, 1905.

W. H. McKinney,
Notary Public.

My Commission expires March 30th, 1909.

Indian Territory,
Central District.

On this the 21 day of October, 1905, personally appeared before me, a notary public in and for the Central District Indian Territory, Silas Pusley and Simom Pusley, and after having been by me first duly sworn according to law say upon their oath that they are over twenty-one years old and that they are citizens of the Choctaw Nation and live about one mile southeast of Damon, I. T. and live about three miles from Green Harvey's. We have known Green Harvey for a period of our natural lives, or since we knew anyone, and know his children, and know when they were born. Clydas Harvey was born on the 20th of July, 1893. We know this to be a fact as we lived near his home when his birth hapened. We have known him ever since,and know him now. He was born before the payment was made in the year 1893 to the Choctaws.

Simon Pusley.
Silas Pusley.

Suscribed and sworn to before me this this the 21 day of October, 1905.

Chas. H. Hudson,
Notary Public.

We Your Committee, to whom was referred the application of Clydas Harvy for his pro rata share of the Leased District fund of $103,00, have to report that we find that Clydas Harvey was born on July 20, 1893, Which was pryor to the date of the payment of this fund to the Choctaw people, and we therefore recommend the following Act.

BE IT ENACTED BY THE GENERAL COUNCIL OF THE CHOCTAW NATION ASSEMBLED.

That the sum of ($103.00) One Hundred and Three Dollars be and the same is hereby appropriated out of any fund in the National Treasury not otherwise appropriated for the purpose of paying Clydas Harvy his share of the Leased District fund, and that the National Auditor shall draw his warrant therefor, and the National Treasurer shall pay the same; and this act shall take effect and be in force from and after its passage and approval.

Proposed by FRANK FOLSOM, Chairman Finance Committee.

Approved this the 30th day of October, 1905.

GREEN McCURTAIN,
P. C. C. N.

BILL NO. 23.

RESOLUTION

ACCEPTING THE REPORT OF GEO. W. SCOTT, NATIONAL TREASURER, FOR THE FISCAL YEAR BEGINNIG OCTOBER 1, 1904, AND ENDING OCTOBER 1, 1905.

Your committee to whom was referred the report of Geo. W. Scott, National Treasurer, for the fiscal year beginning October 1, 1904 and ending October 1, 1905, have carefully examined said report and find that it shows receipts and disbursements as follows:

Total receipts - - -	$157,907.28
Total Disbursements - -	110,769.51
Bal. on hand October 1, 1905,	$47,137.77

We, therefore, recommend the adoption of the following resolution:

BE IT RESOLVED BY THE GENERAL COUNCIL OF THE CHOCTAW NATION ASSEMBLED:

That the annual report of Geo. W. Scott, National Treasurer, for the fiscal year, beginning October 1, 1904, and ending September 30, 1905, be and the same is hereby accepted as true and correct; and that this resolution shall take effect and be in force from and after its passage and approval.

Proposed by FRANK FOLSOM, Chairman Finance Committee.

Approved this the 27th day of November, 1905.

GREEN McCURTAIN,

P. C. C. N.

BILL NO. 24

AN ACT.

FOR THE RELIEF OF RICHARD CROWDER AND OTHERS.

Whereas: It appears, after a thorough investigation that Richard Crowder 58, Van Crowder 50, Thomas C. Crowder 49, Zarabella (Crowder) Goings, 26; Beldon Crowder 22, Fannie Wallis (Crowder) 20, Geo. Crowder 17, Betsy Wright (Crowder) 15, Wm. J. Crowder 48, Abagail Crowder 8, Maggie Crowder 6, Rosie Crowder 4, Wm. H. Crowder 1, Geo. W. Crowder 40 Louisa Crowder 3, Joe Crowder 2, Eli W. Crowder 5, James Crowder 3, and Kate Belle Crowder 1, Choctaws by blood, were entitled to share in the distribution of what was know as the 'Lease District' fund, and

Whereas: For some reason they have not received their pro rata share amounting to one hundred and three dollars ($103.00) each.

THEREFORE.

BE IT ENACTED BY THE GENERAL COUNCIL OF THE CHOCTAW NATION ASSEMBLED.

That the sum of one thousand, nine hundred and fifty-seven dollars be and the same is hereby appropriated out of any money in the National Treasury not otherwise appropriated to pay Richard Crowder aged 58, Van Crowder 50, Thomas C. Crowder 49, Zarabella Goings 26, Bolden Crowder 22, Fannie Wallis 20, Geo. Crowder 17, Betsy Wright 15, Wm. J. Crowder 48, Abagail Crowder 8, Maggie Crowder 6, Rosie Crowder 4, Wm. H. Crowder 1, Geo. W. Crowder 40, LouisaCrowder 3, Loe Crowder 2, Eli W. Crowder 5, James Crowder 3, Kate Belle Crowder 1, who were at the time of the payment of the Leased District Money, in 1893, of the age set opposite their names, their sha re of the Lease District fund:

And the National Auditor is hereby authorized to issue his warrants, and the National Treasurer to pay the same; and this ACT shall take effect and be in force from and after its passage and approval.

Frank Folsom, Chairman Finance Committee.

Approved this the 16th day of November, 1905.

GREEN McCURTAIN,
P. C. C. N.

BILL NO. 26.

RESOLUTION

ACCEPTING THE REPORT OF S. J. HERNDON, COLLECTOR FOR SECOND DISTRICT.

BILL NO. 25.

AN ACT

APPROPRIATING SIXTEEN THOUSAND AND THREE DOLLARS AND NINETY-SEVEN CENTS TO BE PAID TO THE CHICKASAWS AS AGREED UPON.

Whereas: On March 9, 1905, the Commissioners appointed by the Chickasaw and Choctaw Nations for the purpose of making settlement of all claims made by the Chickasaw Nation against the Choctaw Nation, as agreed that all claims should be settled upon the payment by the Choctaw Nation, to theChickasaw Nation, the sum of $16,003.97: and,

Whereas: On June 30, 1905, the Choctaw Council, in Extra Ordinary Session assembled, ratified and conformed the above mentioned agreement: and

Whereas: November 2, 1905, the Legislature of the Chickasaw Nation ratified and confirmed the said agreement and agreed to release the Choctaw Nation from any and all claims as set forth in said agreement upon the payment by the Choctaw Nation of the sum above mentioned.

THEREFORE

BE IT ENACTED BY THE GENERAL COUNCIL OF THE CHOCTAW NATION ASSEMBLED.

That the sum of Sixteen Thousand and Three Dollars and Ninety-Seven Cents ($16,003,97) be and the same is hereby appropriated out of any funds in the National Treasury not otherwise appropriated and the National Auditor is hereby authorized to issue his warrant therefor, and the National Treasurer to pay the same: and this Act shall take effect and be in force from and after its passage and approval.

FRANK FOLSOM, Chairman of Finance Committee.

Approved this the 16th day of November, 1905.

GREEN McCURTAIN,
P. C. C. N.

BILL NO. 26.

RESOLUTION

ACCEPTING THE REPORT OF S. J. HERNDON, COLLECTOR FOR SECOND DISTRICT.

Your Committee, to whom was referred the report of S. J. Herndon, Collector for the Second District, have carefully examined the said report in detail and find that the said S. J. Herndon has turned in to the National Treasury the sum of $2224.24, which said sum is the balance due the Nation from said collector for the time covered by his report.

We, your Committee therefore recommend the adoption of the following resolution:

BE IT RESOLVED BY THE GENERAL COUNCIL OF THE CHOCTAW NATION ASSEMBLED.

That the report of S. J. Herndon, Collector for the Second District of the Choctaw Nation, be and the same is hereby accepted as true and correct, and this resolution shall take effect and be in force from and after its passage and approval.

Proposed by FRANK FOLSOM, Chairman Finance Committee.

Approved this the 16th day of November, 1905.

GREEN McCURTAIN,
P. C. C. N.

BILL NO. 27.

TO THE SENATE AND HOUSE OF REPRESENTATIVES:

GENTLEMEN:—

Your attention is called to the statement, in my last annual message, that the patent controversy had with the Department had been settled, and pursuant to the agreement of our delegate, acting under my instructions, and the Secretary of the Interior, the Commission has transmitted to me for execution one third or more of the patents, and if the work proceeded without further delay the bulk of the patents would be in the hands of the allottees in a short time.

I regret very much to have to advise you that since the writing of that message there has been presented to me for signature only about 100 patents, and at the same time of this last delivery to me, there was handed to me for cancelation about 200 patents that had already been executed by myself, and most of which had been executed by Governor Johnston of the Chickasaw Nation. During this time there has been no patents brought to me for delivery to the allottees as provided by the agreement between myself and the Secretary of the Interior; although I am unofficially informed that many of the patents which have been executed and forwarded to the Department for approval, have been returned to the Commission. As these patents have not been delivered to me I have been unable to deliver them to the allottees; although the delay has not been occasioned by any fault of mine, as I have repeatedly expressed to the Commissioner, Mr. Bixby, my willingness and desire to execute and deliver these patents. According to the treaties I now have only three months in which to execute and deliver all these patents, which is an impossibility, as I could not possibly sign all of these patents in that length of time. Your attention is called to the danger to title which this delay is liable to cause by reason of the fact that the Missouri, Kansas & Texas Railroad is to shortly bring suit in the name of the State of Kansas, for the lands claimed by it through the Choctaw and Chickasaw Nation. I quote for your benefit the opinion of an attorney for the Missouri, Kansas & Texas Railway as follows:

"The bill pending in the Congress of the United States for the admission of Oklahoma and Indian Territory, as a state of the American Union, failed to pass at the last Session. The bill as it passed the House was amended in the Senate, and went to a conference committee of both houses which failed to agree and Congress adjourned without final action. The failure of the measure resulted from a disagreement of the House and Senate as to certain provisions of the bill which provided also for the admission of the territories New Mexico and Arizona.

"It is confidently expected that favorable action will be taken at the coming session, which begins in December, and that the hopes of the people of Oklahoma and Indian Territories, and of your company will be realized by the admission of these territories to statehood.

"Governmental authorities of the state of Kansas have consented to bring suit in the name of that state to test the right of your company, to it's land grant in the Indian Territory. As the grant was to the state of Kansas for the benefit of your company the bringing of the suit will be in its capacity trustee."

Recently Commissioner Bixby suggested to me that I appoint him as my agent for the purpose of delivering to the allottees their patents, representing the United States Government would bear the expense of such delivery should I act upon his suggestion.

On its face this suggestion looks good—but the question comes to my mind; why should the Department come now and make this proposition when it refused to bear the expense of the payment of the townsite money and refused to bear the expense of placing the coal land on sale. Why this suggestion should be made with reference to patents I am at a loss to comprehend. Should you in your wisdom, see proper to favor this manner of delivery, it would relieve me of a very great deal of work, and at the same time relieve the Nation from expense—however, I do not want you to think for a moment that I am desirous of shirking my duty, as I am now, as ever, ready to fulfill my whole duty to my government and my people if I be permitted to do what the law requires me to do.

In conclusion, I would advise that this Council authorize some suitable person to take this and other matters which I shall shortly submit for your consideration direct to the President, and if we fail to get the sympathy and co-operation of the President, we are then at the mercy of the grafter. Respectfully submitted.

GREEN McCURTAIN,
P. C. C. N.

RESOLUTION

AUTHORIZING THE PRINCIPAL CHIEF TO TAKE DEFINITE ACTION TO INSURE THE DELIVERY OF THE PATENTS TO THE ALLOTTEES UNDER THE TREATIES.

Whereas: In a special message addressed to Council, by our Chief Executive on the 16th day of November, 1905, indicates that the agreement entered into by the Honorable Secretary of the Interior and the Chief of the Choctaw Nation, relative to the delivery of patents has not been carried into effect for some reason unknown to our Chief Executive; and

Whereas: Said agreement is fully expressed in a communication from the Honorable Secretary of the Interior to this effect;

"I have no objection to the request made by you,

through your son, and have to advise that the Dawes Commission will be directed to transmit the patents when prepared, direct to you by special messenger, and after the patents have been signed by you they will be transmitted by the messenger of the Dawes Commission to Governor Johnston and when signed by him the messenger will return them to the Dawes Commission to be forwarded to the Department for the approval of the Secretary, through the Commissioner of Indian Affairs, and when approved by the Secretary, will be returned to the Dawes Commission to be recorded and after recording the Commission will send the patents of allotments to Choctaws by messenger to you for delivery to the allottees, and in like manner will transmit to the Governor of the Chickasaw Nation for delivery the patents to the Chickasaw allottees." and

Whereas: During the months of July, August and September, 1905, about 25,000 patents were signed in accordance with agreement aforesaid: and

Whereas: During the latter part of September, 1905, Commissioner Bixby sought to change the above arrangement, presumably on his own motion, and has failed to make any further substantial delivery of patents for proper signature; but has suggested that the Department would deliver the same and pay all expenses incident thereto; and

Whereas, It seems the fixed purpose of the Department, through Commissioner Bixby, not to comply with the above arrangement as agreed on; and,

Whereas; It is the desire of the Choctaw people that the patents be not only delivered speedily, but that same shall be delivered in accordance with the treaty and agreement heretofore mentioned.

THEREFORE.

BE IT RESOLVED BY THE GENERAL COUNCIL OF THE CHOCTAW NATION ASSEMBLED.

That the Principal Chief is hereby authorized to direct out Delegate to Washington, D. C. McCurtain, to lay this matter before the President of the United States, and ask such executive orders as will lead to a speedy delivery of the patents to the allotees entitled to same under the treaties.

Be it further resolved, That the special message heretofore mentioned be hereto attached and made a part of this resolution; and that this resolution shall take effect and be in force from and after its passage and approval.

Proposed by DANIEL WEBSTER, Chairman Committee on Chief's Message.

Approved this the 21st day of November, 1905.

GREEN McCURTAIN
P. C. C. N.

BILL NO. 28.

BE IT ENACTED BY THE GENERAL COUNCIL OF THE CHOCTAW NATION ASSEMBLED:

That the sum of seven thousand five hundred dollars ($7,500) or so much thereof as may be necessary, be and the same is hereby appropriated out of the National Treasury to defray that part of the regular and necessry expenses of the General Council of the Choctaw Nation, incurred at its regular session up to and including October 28, 1905; and this act shall take effect and be in force from and after its passage and approval.

FRANK FOLSOM, Chairman Finance Committee.

Approved this the 26th day of October, 1905.

GREEN McCURTAIN,
P. C. C. N.

BILL NO. 29.
AN ACT

IN RELATION TO SECURING COMPENSATION FROM THE GOVERNMENT OF THE UNITED STATES FOR THE LEASED DISTRICT LANDS.

Whereas: The Choctaws feel that the Government of the United States should, in equity and justice, make a fair compensation to them for the remainder of the "Leased District" lands to which the decision of the Supreme Court of the United States applied in the case of "the Choctaw and Chickasaw Nations vs. the United States and the Wichita and affiliated bands of Indians" since such lands were taken for a wholly inadequated consideration, from the Choctaws and Chickasaws and disposed of by the Government to settlers for a vast sum of money, and

Whereas: Since such decision by the Supreme Court, there remains nothing to be done by the Choctaws and Chickasaws, in the way of securing compensation for such lands except to appeal to the fairness and justness of the Government of the United States; and point out the justice involved in taking, for the slightest compensation, the lands of a helpless people and disposing of them by sale for a vast sum of money to its own citizens.

THEREFORE

BE IT ENACTED BY THE GENERAL COUNCIL OF THE CHOCTAW NATION ASSEMBLED.

That the Principal Chief of the Choctaw Nation be

and he is hereby authorized to employ some competent person or persons to present to the Government of the United States the claim of the Choctaws for compensation for said remaining leased district lands, and to enter into a suitable contract, giving such person or persons full power and authority to represent the Choctaw Nation to that end; and providing for the payment to such person or persons a fair proportion of whatever sum of money may be secured from the United States, as compensation for such service; PROVIDED that such compensation shall be wholly contigent upon recovery and payable only out of the moneys so recovered. And this act shall take effect and be in force from and after its passage and approval.

Approved this the 22nd day of November, 1905.

GREEN McCURTAIN,
P. C. C. N.

BILL NO. 30.

RESOLUTION.

Whereas: By the terms of the Supplementary Agreement, the Citizenship rolls of the Choctaw Nation were closed on September 25, 1902, and no children born of Choctaw Indian parentage thereafter could be enrolled; and

Whereas: Many Indian children have been born since the above date, and whose right to enrollment and participation in the division of tribal property entitled them to favorable consideration; and

Whereas: Certain delinquent Choctaws who have had a tribal status have failed to secure enrollment.

THEREFORE

BE IT RESOLVED BY THE GENERAL COUNCIL OF THE CHOCTAW NATION ASSEMBLED:

Sec. 1. That Congress be requested to enact such

legislation as deemed necessary to enroll Choctaw infants born since March 4, 1905, up to and including March 4, 1906, and such delinquent Choctaws who have an acknowledged tribal status.

Sec. 2. That this resolution shall take effect and be in force from and after its passage and appoval.

Proposed by C. H. JONES.

Approved this the 22nd day of November, 1905.

GREEN McCURTAIN,
P. C. C. N.

BILL NO, 31.

MEMORIAL

To the Congress of the United States:

We, Your Memoralists, the General Council of the Choctaw Nation Assembled, most respectfully represent that we are desirous of extending aid to the old Goodland Presbyterian Missionary School situated at old Goodland, in the Choctaw Nation, Indian Territory.

We further represent that said school is an old institution that has been of incalcuble benefit to the Choctaw people in the upbuilding of the moral character of the Indian youths of the Choctaw Nation. That its religious and educational training has been of the highest order and we memorilists feel that it is appropriate to express our appreciation by respectfully requesting your Honorable Body to appropriate out of the school fund now in the custody of the Government, the sum of five thousand dollars for the use and benefit of the said Old Goodland Presbyterian Missionary school, to the end that we may express our gratitude and appreciation to the institution that has done so much for our people.

Proposed by FRANK FOLSOM, Chairman Finance Committee.

Approved this the 24th day of November, 1905.

GREEN McCURTAIN,
P. C. C. N.

BILL NO. 32.
MEMORIAL

TO CONGRESS RELATING TO THE MURROW INDIAN ORPHANS HOME.

We, your Memorialist in General Council Assembled, respectfully represent that the Murrow Indian Orphans Home is a Non-sectarian Charitable Institution, founded for the purpose of providing a home for the orphan children of Choctaw and Chickasaw parentage, and the old and helpless people of the members of the Choctaw and Chickasaw Nations. The good and charitably inclined people who are laboring to build up this institution are well known for long years throughout the Choctaw and Chickasaw Nations for the benevolent, charitable and spiritual work among the Indians, under the most trying conditions. The Council esteems their work as a labor of love for humanity and believes that some public recognition should be made of these services, and that a suitable amount of land should be donated, in a legal manner, in aiding the maintenance of this institution in order to enable its management to properly care for the unfortunate members of the Choctaw and Chickasaw tribes of Indians in after years. We therefore earnestly recommend that the Congress of the United States enact such legislation as may be deemed appropriate, setting aside the following lands, to-wit:

Sections 18 and 19 in township 2 north, range 12 east; the south half of the northeast quarter; the northeast quarter of the northeast quarter; the south half of the northwest quarter of the northeast quarter; the south half of the southeast quarter; the northeast quarter of the southeast quarter; the south half of the northwest quarter of the southeast quarter; the northeast quarter of the northwest quarter of the southeast quarter; the northeast quarter of the southeast quarter of the southwest quarter and the northwest quarter of the northwest quarter of section 24; and the northwest quarter of the southeast quarter; the north half of the southwest quarter of the southeast quarter; the south half of the southwest quarter of the southwest quarter; the northeast quarter of the southwest quarter of the southwest quarter; and the southeast quarter of the northwest quarter of the southwest quarter of section 23; and the southwest quarter of the southwest quarter of the southeast quarter of section 26; and the southeast quarter of the northwest quarter of the northwest quarter; the south half of the northeast quarter of the northwest quarter; and the northeast quarter of the northeast quarter of the northwest quarter; and the east half of southeast quarter of the northwest quarter of section 25 all in township 2 north range 11 east, containing 1790 acres, as shown by the United States Government survey, for the purposes of said home.

Be it further resolved that this resolution of Council shall take effect and be in force from and after its passage and approval.

J. L. WARD.

Approved this the 24th day of November, 1905.

GREEN McCURTAIN,
P. C. C. N.

BILL NO. 33.

RESOLUTION

ASKING THAT THE LAND OFFICE AT ATOKA AND ARDMORE, WHEN CONSOLIDATED BE LOCATED AT COALGATE. IND. TER.

Whereas; It has been authoratively stated that after January 1, 1906, the land office at Atoka, I. T., and at Ardmore, I. T., would be consolidated into one office; and.

Whereas, As a matter of convenience Coalgate, Ind. Ter., offers more railway facilities for the convenience of the Choctaw and Chickasaw people than either Atoka or Ardmore; and,

Whereas: The people of Coalgate offer to furnish, free of charge, a suitable building and such other accommodations as will suit the convenience of the employees.

THEREFORE

BE IT RESOLVED BY THE GENERAL COUNCIL OF THE CHOCTAW NATION ASSEMBLED.

That Commissioner, Tams Bixby, be most respectfully requested to locate said land office at Coalgate, and that a copy of this resolution be furnished him as conveying the sense of this body; and that this resolution shall take effect and be in force from and after its passage and approval.

Proposed by J. L. WARD.

Approved this the 24th day of November, 1905.

GREEN McCURTAIN,
P. C. C. N.

BILL NO. 34.

MEMORIAL

TO THE CONGRESS OF THE UNITED STATES.

We, your Memorialist, the General Council of the Choctaw Nation Assembled, most respectfully represent that under the terms of the present treaties with the Government our tribal government ends on March 4, 1906.

We further represent that our tribal schools will also close at that time unless remedial legislation is had continuing said schools for the scholastic term. We therefore most respectfully urge such legislation by your body as will continue said tribal schools to the end of the scholastic term on ——— May, 1906.

Proposed by FRANK FOLSOM.

Approved this the 24th day of November, 1905.

GREEN McCURTAIN,
P. C. C. N.

BILL NO. 35.

RECOMMENDING THAT THE CHOCTAW AND CHICKASAW NATIONS BE PERMITTED TO SELL TO JACK GORDON AND HIS ASSOCIATES ONE HUNDRED THOUSAND ACRES OF LAND FOR A GAME PRESERE ONLY.

Whereas: There are thousands of acres of mountaneous and rough lands in the southeastern portion of the Choctaw Nation that can never be of great value as agricultural land; and,

Whereas: It is the desire of Jack Gordon and his associates to purchase one hundred thousand acres of said land, all in one body, at its appraised value; and,

Whereas: There has been very little, if any of the lands that it is desired to sell, that has been allotted by any member of the Choctaw or Chickasaw Tribes of Indians; and,

Whereas: When the selection of this reservation is finally and definitely located, Jack Gordon and his associates express their willingness and intention to satisfactorily settle with all allottees who may be found to have improvements located thereon; and,

Whereas: It is the purpose of this organization to create out of this reservation a game preserve, for the purpose of preserving fish, game and timber; and for no other purpose.

THEREFORE

BE IT RESOLVED BY THE GENERAL COUNCIL OF THE CHOCTAW NATION ASSEMBLED:

That it is the sense of the Choctaw Council that there could be no better disposition made of the lands desired by Jack Gordon and his associates than to dispose of the same at its appraised value; and the Congress of the United States is most earnestly solicited to make the necessary steps looking to the sale of this land to Jack Gordon and his associates at its appraised value —PROVIDED, that if there shall be found to be members of the Choctaw or Chickasaw Tribes of Indians who have selected their allotments within the boundaries of said reserve, who shall express their willingness in writing to release and relinquish their allotments and allot elsewhere, that their allotments be canceled, upon payment by Jack Gordon and his associates satisfactory compensation for the improvements located thereon, and that such allottees be permitted to allot elsewhere—said lands to be set aside and definitely located by a commission consisting of three persons, one to be appointed the by Principal Chief of the Choctaw Nation one to be appointed by the Governor of the Chickasaw Nation, and one to represent Jack Gordon and his associates, whose duty it shall be to locate and to lodge with the Commissioner, at Muskogee, Indian Territory, within ninety days from the date of favorable action upon this measure by the Congress of the United States, legal and definite description of all the lands desired to compose this reservation which it is desired to sell, which shall be all in one body, and that the Congress of the United States shall make suitable provision with reference to payment therefore; and that this resolution shall take effect and be in force from and after its passage and approval.

Proposed by FRANK FOLSOM.

Approved this the 25th day of November, 1905.

GREEN McCURTAIN,
P. C. C. N.

BILL NO. 36.

BE IT ENACTED BY THE GENERAL COUNCIL OF THE CHOCTAW NATION ASSEMBLED.

That the following sums of money are hereby appropriated out of the National Treasury to defray the regular and necessary expenses of the Government for the half fiscal year commencing September 30, 1905, and ending March 4, 1906.

Principal Chief's Salary	$1,000.00
National Secretary's salary	300.00
National Auditor's salary	300.00
National Treasurer's salary	300.00
National Attorney's salary	200.00
Private Secretary's salary	500.00
Trustee, Coal and Asphalt	4,000,00
Nine National Lighthorsemen	700.00
Two Supreme Judges	400.00
Three Circuit Judges	750.00
Seventeen County Judges	2,125.00
Three District Chiefs	75.00
Three District Attorneys	750.00
Grand and Petit Jurors	3,525,00
Witness, Circuit Court	1,500.00
Contingent Fund, Principal Chief	6,162.00
Contingent Fund, National Auditor	400.00
Contingent Fund, Treasurer	400.00
Contingent Fund, Secretary	400.00
Sheriffs and Deputies attending circuit court	675.00
Publication Fund, National Secretary	350.00
Clerk Supreme Court	50.00
Three Circuit Clerks	450.00
Seventeen County Clerks	850.00
Seventeen Sheriffs	2,750.00
Thirty-Four Deputy Sheriffs	1,700.00
Seventeen County Rangers	425.00

Caring for Capitol Building - -	40.00
Delegate to Washington, D. C. -	1,250.00
Expense of Delegate to Washington -	500.00
Expense of attending funeral of Chief Justice Garland - - -	70.60
Expense of General Council from Oct. 29, 1905 to Dec. 1, 1905, both inclusive -	9,000.00
Coal Commissioner - - -	4,000.00

That this act shall take effect and be in force from and after its passage and approval.

Proposed by FRANK FOLSOM, Chairman Finance Committee.

Approved this the 30th day of November, 1905.

GREEN McCURTAIN
P. C. C. N.

BILL NO. 37.

AN ACT.

APPROPRIATING FORTY DOLLARS TO MRS. J. F. MCCURTAIN FOR CLEANING UP THE CAPITOL BUILDING.

Whereas: Owing to the long session of Council the capitol building has become very dirty and should be cleaned up.

THEREFORE

BE IT ENACTED BY THE GENERAL COUNCIL OF THE CHOCTAW NATION ASSEMBLED.

That the sum of forty dollas ($40.00) be and the same is hereby appropriated out of any funds in the National Treasury not otherwise appropriated for the purpose of cleaning the Capitol Building; and that the National Auditor is directed to draw his warrant for said sum, in favor of Mrs. J. F. McCurtain, for said purpose; and the National Treasurer shall pay the same; and this act shall take effect and be in force from and after its passage and approval.

Proposed by FRANK FOLSOM, Chairman Finance Committee.

Approved this the 26th day of October, 1905.

GREEN McCURTAIN,
P. C. C. N

BILL NO. 38.

RESOLUTION

ACCEPTING THE REPORT OF PETER J. HUDSON, NATIONAL AUDITOR.

We, your Committee, to whom was referred the report of Peter J. Hudson, National Auditor, for the fiscal year ending September 30, 1905, have carefully examined same and find it true and correct, and therefore recommend the adoption of the following resolution:

BE IT RESOLVED BY THE GENERAL COUNCIL OF THE CHOCTAW NATION ASSEMBLED.

Sec. 1. That the report of Peter J. Hudson, National Auditor, for the fiscal year ending September 30, 1905, be and the same is hereby accepted as true and correct; and that this resolution shall take effect and be in force from and after its passage and approval.

Proposed by FRANK FOLSOM, Chairman Finance Committee.

Approved this the 27th day of November, 1905.

GREEN McCURTAIN,
P. C. C. N.

BILL NO. 39.

RESOLUTION

ENDORSING HONORABLE GEORGE K. PRITCHARD, UNITED STATES MARSHAL FOR THE CENTRAL DISTRICT INDAIN TERRITORY.

Whereas: The Choctaw people are vitally interested in the enforcement of the law in the Choctaw Nation; and

Whereas: Honorable George K. Pritchard, United States Marshal for the Central District of the Indian Territory, has, since his incumbency, filled that responsible position with entire satisfaction to the whole people of the Choctaw Nation; and

Whereas: We feel it proper to endorse and warmly commend his record in this respect.

THEREFORE.

BE IT RESOLVED BY THE GENERAL COUNCIL OF THE CHOCTAW NATION ASSEMBLED.

That the thanks of this body be extended to Honorable George K. Pritchard, United States Marshal for his uniform enforcement of the law and his manifest determination to apply but one standard to those who violate its precepts.

Be it further resolved that this resolution take effect and be in force from and after its passage and approval.

Proposed by FRANK FOLSOM.

Approved this the 25th day of November, 1905.

GREEN McCURTAIN,
P. C. C. N.

BILL NO. 40.

RESOLUTION

ENDORSING JUDGE THOMAS C. HUMPHREY.

Whereas: Judge Thomas C. Humphrey, United States Judge for the Central District of the Indian Territory has excited the respect of the Choctaw people by his enforcement of the probate laws of the Choctaw Nation; and,

Whereas; His virgorous utterances from the bench indicate his full determination to exterminate the grafter and his nefarious practices in the Choctaw Nation.

THEREFORE

BE IT RESOLVED BY THE GENERAL COUNCIL OF THE CHOCTAW NATION ASSEMBLED.

Sec. 1. That the General Council of the Choctaw Nation Assembled return a vote of thanks to Judge Thomas C. Humphrey for the above reasons, and that a copy of the above resolution be forwarded him as the sense of this body; and that this resolution shall take effect and be in force from and after its passage and approval.

Proposed by J. L. WARD.

Approved this the 25th day of November, 1905.

GREEN McCURTAIN,
P. C. C. N.

BILL NO. 41.

RESOLUTION.

RESPONDING TO A SPECIAL MESSAGE OF THE PRINCIPAL CHIEF CONCERNING THE SALE OF THE COAL AND ASPHALT LANDS AND DEPOSITS OF THE CHOCTAW AND CHICKASAW NATIONS.

Whereas: The Principal Chief, by Special Message, submitted at the regular October session of the General Council, Nov. 21, 1905, has asked this body for an expression of its view as to the best and most advantageous way of selling the coal and asphalt lands and deposits of the Choctaw and Chickasaw Nations; and,

Whereas; The Principal Chief, in his special message referred to an unofficial offer of $15,000,000 for the entire coal and asphalt interests of the Choctaw and Chickasaw Nations, indicating the temper of the market for said coal and asphalt property as a whole, which amount far exceeds in average price per acre, the offers heretofore made under sealed bids; and,

Whereas, The present plan of selling the coal and asphalt lands and deposits by sealed bids has utterly failed to dispose of said lands, or any part of them ;and

Whereas: It is well known that the leased coal and asphalt lands and deposits are far superior in value to the unleased lands and deposits.

THEREFORE

BE IT RESOLVED BY THE GENERAL COUNCIL OF THE CHOCTAW NATION ASSEMBLED:

That, in response to the Special Message of the Principal Chief requesting an expression of the Council as to the best and most advantageous way of selling the coal and asphalt lands and deposits of the Choctaw-Chickasaw Nations, we hereby declare our opposition to the present methods of selling said lands for the folowing reasons:

First. Sale by sealed bids has proved a failure for the reason among other things, that it does not excite competition in bidding.

Second. We are opposed to putting all our inferior coal lands on the market, that is the unleased coal lands, to the exclusion of our superior lands; that is, the leased coal lands, for the reason that the price that will be paid for our inferior coal lands will set a low precedent for our best coal lands, and thereby exert an improper and damaging influence on our coal market.

Third. We are opposed to restricting the sale of our coal lands to nine hundred and sixty acre tracts, for the reason that it shuts the small purchaser out of the market entirely, and on the other hand the large purchaser is not attracted because it does not permit him to buy as much as he might want.

Fourth. We are opposed to the present manner of the sale of our coal lands for the reason that it does not sufficiently advertise said properties.

We would therefore suggest, and in suggesting we would direct the officers of our government in the same, that an effort be made to get a change in the manner of sale of said coal and asphalt lands and deposits so that:

1st: Whoever sells said land and deposits shall have authority to sell them either at public auction or private sale according as the interest will be best protected, and that in either event the purchase price shall be approved by the President before acceptance.

2nd. That the leased and unleased coal lands be put on the market without discrimination one against the other.

3rd. That said coal lands be sold in any amount not less than forty acres, to suit the purchaser: PROVIDED, always, that the best price obtainable shall control this discretion.

4th. That the coal lands and deposits be good and sufficiently advertised to insure a fair sale of the same and that this resolution shall take effect and be in force from and after its passage and approval.

Proposed by DANIEL WEBSTER, Chairman Committee on Chief's Message.

Approved this the 25th day of November, 1905.

GREEN McCURTAIN,
P. C. C. N.

BILL NO, 42.
MEMORIAL

ASKING CONGRESS TO ENACT A GAME LAW EFFECTIVE IN INDIAN TERRITORY.

Whereas: The destruction of game now in progress in the Choctaw Nation is of such a character that unless some relief is afforded game will entirely disappear; and,

Whereas: The present law seems wholly inadequate to protect the game from hunters who flock here from the States without let or hinderance from any source.

THEREFORE.

BE IT RESOLVED BY THE GENERAL COUNCIL OF THE CHOCTAW NATION ASSEMBLED.

That Congress be earnestly requested to enact a law forbidding the further destruction of game under such penalties as may be deemed proper, and that this resolution shall take effect and be in force from and after its passage and approval.

Proposed by FRANK FOLSOM.

Approved this the 28th day of November, 1905.

GREEN McCURTAIN,
P. C. C. N.

BILL NO. 43.

TO THE HON. ETHAN ALLEN HITCHCOCK, SECRETARY OF THE INTERIOR:

The General Council of the Choctaw Nation assembled most respectfully represent that under the Atoka agreement, concluded between the United States government and the Choctaw and Chickasaw Nations, it was agreed that all the funds due the members comprising said Nations were to be capitalized and paid to the members thereof as soon as practicable, after the expiration of tribal government. We further represent that we realize that a full settlement cannot be had at this time, by reason of the fact that the coal and asphalt lands yet remain to be sold, as well as the surplus lands, together with the funds accruing from the sale of town lots and public buildings, not yet being available for this purpose. We respectfully suggest, however: The trust funds and all other funds that have been placed to the credit of the Choctaw and Chickasaw people up to date be paid out per capita at the earliest possible date. This suggestion is prompted by the knowledge of the true condition of the Choctaw and Chickasaw allottees, who are striving to build homes and otherwise improve their allotments.

We respectfully represent that a favorable action by the Department upon this suggestion herein contained would do much to encourage the full-blood Indians who are trying to abandon the customs and traditions that have retarded their progress in the past, and are making a sincere effort to keep pace with the progress and enlightenment that a change in the land tenure has forced upon them.

Proposed by S. W. MAYTUBBY.

Approved this the 28th day of November, 1905.

GREEN McCURTAIN,
P. C. C. N.

BILL NO. 44.

RESOLUTION

TAKING RECESS OF COUNCIL UNTIL JANUARY 29, 1906.

BE IT RESOLVED BY THE GENERAL COUNCIL OF THE CHOCTAW NATION ASSEMBLED:

That this Conncil take a recess on December 1, 1905, until January 29, 1906, unless sooner directed to assemble by the Principal Chief; and that this resolution take effect and be in force from and after its passage and approval.

Proposed by FRANK FOLSOM.

Approved this the 27th day of November, 1905.

GREEN McCURTAIN
P. C. C. N.

BILL NO. 45.

AN ACT

CREATING A BOARD OF COMMISSIONERS WITH AUTHORITY TO REPRESENT THE CHOCTAW PEOPLE IN ALL MATTERS AFFECTING THEIR INTERSTS AS A TRIBE AFTER THE EXPIRATION OF THE TRIBAL GOVERNMENT.

Whereas: By the terms of the Atoka Agreement, Section 29 of the act of Congress approved June 28, 1898 (30 Stat. 495) the Choctaw tribal government was continued for a period of eight years from March 4, 1898, in order to carry out the requirements of said agreement; and,

Whereas: By the same terms of said agreement the tribal government will expire March 4, 1906, without having had an opportunity to fully accomplish the purpose for which it was continued; and,

Whereas: There are yet remaining unsettled and undisposed of many matters in which the Choctaw people as a tribe have a deep interest such as providing for the sale of the surplus or residue lands and the execution of patents therefore; the final allotment of said land and the issuance of patents to those Mississippi Choctaws who make proof of their right to receive the same, and the contesting of the claims of other Mississippi Choctaws who may have forfeited their rights under the law to receive final allotments of land; the execution of patents and the delivery thereof to allottees who have not received their patents; the execution of patents to town lots on which final payments are not yet due; the sale of school lands and buildings and other public property and the execution of proper title thereto, etc., and in all of which it is right and proper that the Choctaw people should have re resentation; and,

Whereas: It is not the policy of the Government of the United States or the desire of the Choctaw people to continue the tribal government beyond the time agreed upon, it therefore becomes expedient under the unsettled condition of things that tribal authority or reprensetation of some kind be continued until all matters of interest to the Choctaw people as a tribe are finally and successfully wound up.

THEREFORE

BE IT ENACTED BY THE GENERAL COUNCIL OF THE CHOCTAW NATION ASSEMBLED.

Sec. 1. That a board of Commissioners be and the the same is hereby created with authority to represent the Choctow people in all matters effecting their community or tribal interests after the expiration of the tribal government.

Sec. 6 That such board of commissioners shall be composed of three persons who shall be citizens by blood of the Choctaw Nation, and said board shall consist of a chairman, vice-chairman and secretary. That the present Principal Chief, Green McCurtain, be and he is hereby made a member of said board, and by this act constituted chairman thereof, with the authority to appoint the other two members who shall be made vice-chairman and secretary respectively.

Sec. 3. That it is the will and desireof the Choctaw people hereby expressed that the chairman of the board of commissioners herein provided for shall exercise all the authority vested in him as Principal Chief by the terms of the Atoka and Supplementary Agreements. That in the event of death, resignation or inability for any cause of any member of said board to serve, then the remaining commissioners shall have the power to fill such vacancy.

Sec. 4. That in all other matters affecting the interests of the tribe in which it may become necessary or proper that the Choctaw people be represented, wherein the tribe is by the present law allowed representation; in defending the tribal interests against unlawful claims of Mississippi Choctaws to final allotments of land; the sale of the residue of unallotted lands; the sale of town lots, etc., the board of Commissioners or a majority thereof shall represent the Choctaw people and take whatever steps in their judgement are necessary to adequately protect the interests of the tribe.

Sec. 5. That the terms of office of the members of the board of commissioners shall begin with the expiration of the tribal government, March 4, 1906, and continue until all matters of tribal interests are finally settled and disposed of. That the salary of the members of the board of commissioners shall be five thousand dollars each per annum, together with all regular and necessary expenses not to exceed two thousand dollars per annum for each member of the board. That the Choctaw people hereby consent to the payment of the salary and expenses of the board of commissioners from the funds on deposit with the United States Government belonging to the tribe, upon the order of the President.

Sec. 6. That this act is amendatory to such of the acts now in force relative to the final settlement of matters affecting the interests of the Choctaw Nation; and that this act shall take effect when approved by the President, and be in force from and after March 4th 1906.

Proposed by FRANK FOLSOM.

Approved this the 25th day of November, 1905.

GREEN McCURTAIN

P. C. C. N.

BILL NO. 46.

AN ACT

FOR THE RELIEF OF DAISY FISHER MULDROW AND OTHERS.

We, your committee to whom was referred the petition of Daisy Fisher Muldrow, Agnes Fisher Colbert and Blanche Fisher, children of D. O. Fisher, and acknowledged citizens of the Choctaw Nation, requesting that they be allowed their pro rata share in the "Leased District" fund, do find, after a thorough investigation of the facts, that the petitioners are entitled to relief, and we therefore recommend the passage of the following act:

BE IT ENACTED BY THE GENERAL COUNCIL OF THE CHOCTAW NATION ASSEMBLED.

That the sum of three hundred and nine dollars ($309.00) be and the same is hereby appropriated out of any funds in the National Treasury not otherwise appropriated, for the purpose of paying Daisy Fisher Muldrow, AgnesFisher Colbert and Blanche Fisher their pro rata share of the Leased District fund, amounting to one hundred and three dollars ($103.00) each.

Be it further enacted, that the National Auditor is hereby authorized to issue his warrant and the National Treasurer pay the same, and this act shall take effect and be in force from and after its passage and approval by the President.

Proposed by FRANK FOLSOM, Chairman Finance Committee.

Approved this the 29th day of November, 1905.

GREEN McCURTAIN,

P. C. C. N.

BILL NO. 47.

AN ACT

CREATING AN AUDITING BOARD, AND FOR OTHER PURPOSES.

Whereas: In view of the end of tribal government and the necessity of effecting a final settlement in the various counties and districts of the Choctaw Nation, and ascertaining their exact indebtedness, if any, and

Whereas: The creation of some central authority for this purpose is deemed advisable and necessary.

THEREFORE

BE IT ENACTED BY THE GENERAL COUNCIL OF THE CHOCTAW NATION ASSEMBLED.

Section 1. That George W. Scott, Treasurer, Peter J. Hudson, Auditor, E. H. Wilson, National Secretary, and V. M. Everidge, National Attorney, are hereby named as an auditing board for the purpose of ascertaining the exact financial condition of the various counties and districts of the Choctaw Nation That said board shall convene at Tuskahoma, I. T., within twenty days after the passage and approval of this act for the purpose of organization, and shall at that time notify the various county and district clerks of the Choctaw Nation to make a report of the condition of their respective counties and districts.

Sec. 2. That said board is hereby authorized to organize by electing a president and secretary; and that it shall be the duty of said board to take up and cancel all genuine outstanding county scrip, and to issue in its stead certificates signed by the President and Secretary of said board, which shall entitle the holder thereof to a National warrant upon presentation of the same to the National Auditor.

Sec. 3. The said board shall convene on February 5, 1906, and shall receive and receipt each county and district clerk for all the county and district property held by them; and it shall be the duty of the county clerks and treasurers of the various counties of the Choctaw Nation to turn over to the National Treasurer all funds in their possession, including the $50 allowed by law; and all books, records and papers of whatever kind in the custody of the county and district clerks shall be lodged in the office of the National Secretary for safe keeping.

Sec. 4. That the compensation of said board shall be $5 per day each, when actually engaged in the service herein provided.

Sec. 5. That the sum of five hundred dollars, or so much thereof as may be necessary, shall be made available, and upon the certificate of the Principal Chief the National Auditor shall issue his warrant and the National Treasurer shall pay the same. That the contingent fund of the Principal Chief is hereby sufficiently increased to carry into effect the provisions of this act; and this act shall take effect and be in force from and after its passage and approval.

Proposed by W. A. DURANT.

Approved this the 29th day of November, 1905.

GREEN McCURTAIN,
P. C. C. N.

BILL NO. 48.

AN ACT

REPEALING AN ACT ENTITLED "FOR THE RELIEF OF MRS. J. F. M'CURTAIN FOR CLEANING THE CAPITOL."

BE IT ENACTED BY THE GENERAL COUNCIL OF THE CHOCTAW NATION ASSEMBLED.

That the act of Nov. 27, 1905, appropriating $40 in favor of Mrs. J. F. McCurtain for cleaning the capitol building be and the same is hereby repealed; and this act shall take effect and be in force from and after its passage and approval.

E. A. MOORE.

Approved this the 28th day of November, 1905.

GREEN McCURTAIN,
P. C. C. N.

BILL NO. 49.

AN ACT

REPEALING AN ACT ENTITLED "AN ACT TO DEFRAY THE EXPENSES OF THE COMMITTEE APPOINTED TO ATTEND THE FUNERAL OF CHIEF JUSTICE GARLAND.

BE IT ENACTED BY THE GENERAL COUNCIL OF THE CHOCTAW NATION ASSEMBLED.

That the act of October 24, 1905 appropriating $70.60, the expenses of the committee who attended the funeral of Chief Justice Garland, be and the same is hereby repealed, and this act shall take effect and be in force from and after its passage and approval.

Proposed by W. A. DURANT.

Approved this the 29th day of November, 1905.

GREEN McCURTAIN,
P. C. C. N.

BILL NO. 50.

RESOLUTION.

REPEALING THE RESOLUTION OF ADJOURNMENT DESIGNATING DEC. 1, 1905.

BE IT RESOLVED BY THE GENERAL COUNCIL OF THE CHOCTAW NATION ASSEMBLED:

That the resolution of adjournment passed by this Council designating Dec. 1, 1905, as the date of the final adjournment of the regular session of the October Term of Council, 1905, be and the same is hereby repealed;

and this resolution shall take effect from and after its passage and approval.

Proposed by W. A. DURANT.

Became a law by limitation December 11, 1905.

THIS IS TO CERTIFY, That the above and foregoing is a full, true and correct copy of the Original Acts and Resolutions of the Choctaw General Council, passed at its Extraordinary and at it's Regular Session for the year 1905, the Originals whereof are now on file in the office of the National Secretary of said Nation.

IN TESTIMONY WHEREOF, I, Edward H. Wilson, National Secretary of said Nation, have hereunto affixed my official signature and the Seal of the Choctaw Nation. Done this 17th day of January, in the year One Thousand Nine Hundred and Six.

EDWARD H. WILSON,

SEAL.] National Secretary Choctaw Nation.

INDEX

PAGE

PART ONE.

PART TWO.